Food Magic

FOOD MAGIC

Easy Ideas for Pretty Dishes

CAROL PASTOR

CASSELL

This book is dedicated to two fine chefs
Colin Campbell and Thomas Everest − my grandfathers

First published in the UK 1995 by
Cassell Publishers Ltd
Wellington House
125 Strand
London WC2R 0BB

Distributed in Australia by Capricorn Link (Australia) Pty Ltd
2/13 Carrington Road, Castle Hill, NSW 2154

British Library Cataloguing in Publication Data
A catalogue record for this book is available from
the British Library

ISBN 0–304–34423–0

Printed and bound in Slovenia

CONTENTS

INTRODUCTION

Food is infinitely more attractive when it is presented with style. A little ornament to invite the eye and mind into delicious anticipation; a garnish of feathery dill to emphasize the delicacy of poached fish; a tiny pastry bow, a rosette of meringue or whipped cream; a tiny, gem-like tartlet, dusted with icing sugar – all contrive to tempt the eye and restore the palate of the most jaded guest.

It is said that a well-known Knightsbridge restaurant prospered because it displayed exotic flowers with every course. One London hotel even served a giant birthday cake strapped precariously to the back of a baby elephant. In Harrods Food Hall we can see food presentation at its best and most inventive: pâtés sporting pimento flowers and cucumber leaves, sealed in clear, sparkling layers of aspic that glitters like diamonds; fresh fruits built into pyramids of layered colours interleaved with shiny green bay leaves; kirsch-flavoured marzipan shaped into chestnuts at Christmas; raised game pies, massive and golden, with shiny glazed fleurons; pesto, tomato and walnut breads, swirled together in ingenious tri-coloured plaits.

While it is unlikely that many of us would wish to scale such culinary heights, we might be eager to find inspiration to bring the stamp of creative originality to our dinner and supper parties that will make them memorable far beyond that last morsel of dessert.

We could spend hours searching through the grand food emporia or gazing into the windows of the finest patisseries. We could look for inspiration in cookery books or glossy food magazines or eat in innovative restaurants and take some of the ideas home with us. We can, however, also adapt and create in our own kitchen. With patience and culinary ingenuity we can produce creative food with a casual elegance, whether it is served in a formal dining room or on a well-worn pine table in a country kitchen.

Often, what looks best is the simplest to prepare. Foods such as freshly picked garden vegetables and fruit are enhanced by natural presentation – a garnish of single fresh leaves or a flower; a bowl of peas with small, whole peapods mixed in and finished off with a single stem of pea flowers. What is most natural can be most pleasing and creative. The lovely speckled shells of tiny, hard-boiled quails' eggs look particularly eye-catching presented in a nest of reindeer moss, with a few token feathers stuck around the edge. The edible petals of orange marigolds, purple violets and bright yellow and orange nasturtiums make a dazzling addition to the salad bowl.

A simple mandarin and rosemary jelly is served on a majolica plate and decorated with nasturtiums, picked fresh from the garden.

Other recipes can be contrived to place the emphasis on creative presentation, although these are not, perhaps, the kind of dishes to whip up on a normal evening. A poached salmon, for example, delicately coated with aspic and decorated with scales formed from crescents of cucumber, is not an everyday dish.

Moulding shapes can sometime elevate quite simple food into a glamorous centrepiece. A fish mousse made in a tin shaped like a scallop shell will look even more handsome with strands of tender green chives arranged to outline the ribs radiating from the apex of the shell; an airy custard-like *crème brûlée*, finished with a caramelized sugar, glazed as smooth as glass, can be sealed inside pretty china heart-shaped dishes.

The china and table accessories you use are important, too, and can often make food more fun to eat. A Carlton Ware cucumber plate looks wonderful with glistening green slices of vegetable set upon it, but it will do equally well as a container for scarlet radish roses and spring onions or for a single line of grilled goat's cheeses. Leaf-patterned china dishes make exquisite serving dishes for peas, broad beans and young vegetables. Even if you do not like oysters, some oyster plates are quite beautiful, with their elaborate patterns of fish, crustaceans and scallop and conch shells. You can use them for a dish called salagmundy, which is a delicious concoction of fish and meat titbits. Many a fishy delicacy, arranged around the central depression, which can be filled with a dipping sauce, will look pretty on one of these plates. If you break the lid of a large, beautiful tureen, don't hide the bottom half away in a cupboard – it will make a fine flower vase or, filled with crushed ice, a splendid chiller for champagne flutes.

Years ago the British pottery company Minton was among the first to appreciate the importance of presenting food attractively. The company produced china with relief patterns dedicated to natural themes – birds, flowers, fish and fruit – that both evoked and anticipated the real foods that would be served upon it. Dishes were designed with motifs of wild strawberries and tiny wells for cream. Fish platters were ornamented with patterns of crustaceans, shells and oyster shells. One dish even had a life-size, shiny, glazed silver-grey fish as a handle of an elegant terrine, and when the lid was lifted, there would be lying the 'real thing', ready to be eaten. The Minton archives include dusty shelves piled high with portfolios filled by artists working on designs for food-related china.

However simple it is, food looks better on the right plate. This was the simple rule that guided Minton, and it will also be the basis for the inspiration for this book.

A simple yet elegant presentation for a toothsome vanilla, ginger, honey and saffron ice-cream bombe.

AFTERNOON TEA

It would be impossible to taste every tea grown in the world. China alone recognizes more than 2,000 different types of leaf, and it is drunk in some form almost everywhere in the world. I decided to begin my search for the perfect afternoon cup in one of the best known specialist shops in Britain, Imperial Teas of Lincoln, and I arranged to meet tea man *extraordinaire* Ben Poole there. The establishment is situated high on Steep Hill, a picturesque cobbled street running steeply down from the old part of this lovely cathedral city to the new. The Poole family shop, which is run by Ben and his brothers Mark and James, has flagstone floors and half-timbered, sloping walls. A maze of shelves is laden with polished silver samovars, teapots and other tea-making paraphernalia jostling with over 300 Chinese tea caddies, all holding different kinds of tea. The teas range from the fairly standard Ceylon tea from the Lover's Leap Estate to the grandest and rarest, exotic Silver Needles, which had been sent to Ben the very week we met from a mist- and fog-bound island in Hunan Province. This tea is unusual because the needle-shaped leaves stand on end

A beautiful Minton tea plate designed by William Stephen Coleman in 1869.

close to the surface of the hot water instead of sinking to the bottom, as tea leaves normally do. Ben and I spent a happy afternoon sipping and discussing the delights of this delicious and versatile beverage.

Whichever tea you choose, make it with the care it deserves. Add the tea leaves to a properly heated pot and use freshly drawn water, which must be boiling as it is added to the pot – take the pot to the kettle, as the saying has it. Cover the pot and allow the leaves

to inflate in the hot liquid. How long you leave it depends on the type of leaf, but generally 3 minutes will suffice. Some teas, particularly green teas and tisanes, become bitter with prolonged brewing. Some teapots are designed to prevent the tea from over-brewing.

LUXURIOUS AFTERNOON BLEND
For four people add to a heated teapot 1 large, rounded teaspoon of Darjeeling, which has a fine, distinctive flavour, 1 level teaspoon of fragrant Earl Grey and 1 level teaspoon of a light China tea, such as Keemun, which has a slightly sweet, malty taste. Fill the pot with boiling water and allow the leaves to infuse for about 3 minutes. Drink with milk and sugar if liked.

ASSAM AND CEYLON
Blended together, these make a mellow tea with a good colour. Place 1 teaspoon of each in a heated pot, add boiling water and leave to stand for 3 minutes. Drink as it is or add milk and sweeten with sugar if preferred.

Delicate porcelain bowls hold a variety of exciting teas from which your guests can choose for themselves.

A picture made largely of teas and inspired by Minton's No. 1 pattern book.

OOLONG

This is a lovely, brightly coloured tea with a lively flavour. It makes a wonderful teatime beverage, which is also healthy because it contains a natural anti-oxidant that is twenty times more effective that vitamin E. Try it as it is or with added fruit oils, such as peach blossom. You can drink it with milk if you wish, but I think it tastes nicer without. Add sugar if preferred.

EARL GREY

This tea contains bergamot, an oil made from the Canton orange. The best grade of oil of bergamot does not have as strong an odour as the artificial oils used by some tea manufacturers to flavour their teas. The tea was named because its secret formula was said to have been disclosed by a Chinese mandarin to Earl Grey in 1830. When he returned to Britain, the Earl had it re-created by a tea merchant in London. Its fragrant, slightly citrus bouquet makes it perfect for afternoon drinking.

Try blending Earl Grey with Orange Blossom Oolong to make an equally delicious, soothing drink. Add sugar if you wish, but the flavour can usually best be appreciated without milk.

Earl Grey can also be served with a twist of citrus. The leaves can be mixed with mallow flowers, lemon peel, lemon grass and lemon verbena – anything, in fact, that begins with lemon – to make a delightful afternoon drink with a real zing.

PAI MU TAN

Apart from being a health-giving beverage, this is the perfect tea to serve in an arrangement of different teas because the whole green leaves still bear the white hairs that are the natural down on the young, untreated leaves, which are not fomented like black tea.

FRUIT AND FLOWER TEAS

These teas have a fruity or flowery taste, evocative of summer, and they make a pleasant afternoon drink. They are sometimes bought for their attractive appearance as well as for their flavour, and they are ideal for a tea presentation, when the rainbow combination of coloured flower petals and strips of brightly coloured fruit zests mingle with dark tea. Sweeten to taste, but definitely no milk.

TISANES

Most people think of tisanes as teas. In fact, they are not teas at all, the only similarity lying in the method in which they are made – by infusing fruit, flowers or leaves in hot water. Cookery books say you can make your own by drying flower petals and fruit segments in summer, but after several rather disappointing attempts at making my own, I discovered that the flavours of home-made tisanes are not nearly as pronounced as the shop-bought ones, which have essentials oils added to the fruits and flowers. Ben Poole agreed with me on this point, but added that tea men do not like tisanes anyway. Camomile and mint do have strong flavours and would make good infusions. Try drying them gently on a hot day but out of the sun, finishing off in an airing-cupboard if necessary. Once they are bone dry, store them in air-tight tins.

To prepare an infusion, place several teaspoonfuls in boiling water and leave for 2 minutes to produce a flowery or fruity liquid with a pale colour and delicate aroma. They make a pleasant afternoon drink that only requires sweetening to taste.

Incidentally, rock candy crystal sugar sweetens without flavouring tea (see page 80), and it is especially good to use in the more highly scented teas and tisanes.

HOT LEMON TEA

Early in the nineteenth century the Minton factory produced a set of fine china tea wares consisting of an overall pattern of cut orange and lemon slices against a background of purple and lemon leaves, and this set from the past is a reminder of how good tea tastes with a hint of citrus to make a really refreshing drink on a hot summer's day.

Make a lighter brew than usual with a black tea, such as Ceylon, Darjeeling or Keemun, and serve it very hot with one thin slice of lemon or, if you wish, lime or orange, per person, without milk but with a little sugar if wished.

COLD LEMON TEA

This is another drink ideally suited to hot afternoons, particularly if you are taking your tea alfresco. Add 1 teaspoon of tea (try Earl Grey with oil of bergamot) to a 600ml (1 pint) jug. Fill with cold water and leave in the fridge overnight. Decant into another clear glass jug and top up with two slices of lemon, ice cubes and sprigs of fresh mint leaves. Drink without milk but sweeten with sugar if preferred.

MINT TEA

Mint tea is an unusual and invigorating afternoon drink, with just a hint of exotic Arabia. Make a brew of Gunpowder tea, which is instantly recognizable because its young leaves are rolled into tiny, pellet-like balls. Add finely chopped mint leaves, using spearmint or Moroccan mint for a really strong flavour, and sweeten well. Serve this fairly condensed sweet liquid very hot in small tea glasses. This uplifting, amber-golden beverage has a very special flavour. Drink it without milk.

A Minton majolica glazed earthenware teapot, c.1865.

ASPIC DECORATION FOR MEAT AND FISH

The Concise Encyclopedia of Gastronomy (published by the Wine and Food Society, 1993) tells us that aspic – the name comes from the French word for meat jelly – was so named because one of the pot herbs used for flavouring the bone stock was called 'espic' or 'spikenard'. Elaborate patterns can be made with carefully cut vegetable pieces, carefully arranged to decorate the jewel-like aspic.

A single *oeuf en gelée*, for example, in which a small poached or soft-boiled egg is suspended inside a moulded dome of well-flavoured aspic, requires a superior tasting bone stock and careful clarification if it is to work. However, this process can take hours, and it is not necessarily appropriate for every aspic dish. Buffet dishes of meats or fish require only a thin shiny coat to preserve them attractively, and they could use a simpler recipe with the aspic flavoured with vegetable stock and a touch of sherry.

BASIC ASPIC

Add 1.75 litres/3 pints of water and 1 tsp of salt to a large saucepan. Add the white parts of 2 leeks, 2 onions and 6 peppercorns to the stockpot. Bring to the boil and leave to simmer for about 45 minutes until the liquid has reduced to about 600ml/1 pint. Strain it twice through a scalded jelly bag or a folded piece of muslin into a measuring jug. Top up the liquid with a little extra water to 600ml/1 pint if necessary and place it in a saucepan. (If you wish to clarify the stock, do so at this point; see below.) Heat the stock but do not boil. Remove it from the heat and half-fill a teacup with hot stock. Sprinkle into the teacup 25g/1oz of gelatine powder and stir briskly until it has dissolved. Stir the liquid gelatine into the hot vegetable stock in the saucepan. Leave to cool a little, then stir in 2½ tbs of pale sherry. Chill in the fridge for 30 minutes, then cool the aspic on top of ice, stirring with a spoon until the mixture begins to look thick and syrupy, rather like thick oil. It is now ready to use. If it sets too quickly, you can warm the aspic briefly over a bowl of hot water, chilling it again over ice and stirring it with a spoon until the liquid reverts to a thick, oily consistency.

Decorative Aspic

If you want to add colour and pattern to clear aspic with an arrangement of small cut vegetables, you will need a very sharp knife and some small aspic cutters, although on larger items of food it is sometimes better to make free-form decorations.

Cover the food with a first layer of aspic and chill, keeping the remaining aspic at room temperature. If the aspic sets, remelt it as before. Have your vegetable decorations ready and dip each one into a saucer of aspic, before using a pointed knife to set it carefully in place on the surface of the aspic-covered food. When you are satisfied with the arrangement, spoon over another thin layer to cover the decorations. Chill to set.

Clarifying Aspic

Lightly whisk together 2 egg whites with a fork, then whisk this into the cold stock as you bring it to the boil. At this point you can also add the broken shells of two eggs. As it boils, remove the whisk to allow all the substances that have become attached to the egg white and shells to rise to the surface. Allow to cool slightly before passing through a fine sieve, two layers of cheesecloth or a scalded jelly bag.

CHICKEN CHAUDFROID

This dish is a glorified poached chicken bathed in a coat of white bechamel sauce, which is coated in decorated aspic. This is not an everyday dish, although, taken step by step, it is quite easy and chicken breasts are easier to manage than the whole bird.

SERVES 6

INGREDIENTS
850ml/1½pt chicken stock (see below)
6 pieces chicken breast, wing bone attached
seasoning

SAUCE
55g/2oz butter
55g/2oz plain flower
450ml/¾pt (taken from the stock in which you poach the chicken)
12g/½oz powdered gelatine

ASPIC
300ml/½pt chicken stock, cleared with
1 egg white and shell (see page 12)
1½ tsp powdered gelatine

DECORATION
tarragon leaves
black olives, pitted
red pepper, skinned or carrot, thinly sliced

Make the bone stock by adding the same vegetables that are used in the vegetable stock (see page 12) to 1 large raw chicken carcass and 2.25l/4pt water in a large saucepan, simmered together until reduced to 850ml/1½pt stock.

Heat the chicken stock in a medium sized saucepan. Season the chicken breasts and put them into the stock. Leave to simmer gently for 5-6 minutes. Remove the chicken with a slotted spoon, cover with plastic film and leave to cool before placing in the fridge.

Make the sauce by melting the butter in a small saucepan. Add the flour and cook gently, stirring continuously until the roux leaves the side of the pan. Add 450ml/¾pt chicken stock (substituting 150ml/¼pt milk for the same amount of stock to make a whiter sauce), passed through a fine sieve lined with muslin, to the roux in a slow stream, stirring over a low heat until it is silky smooth. Sprinkle the gelatine over 3 tbsp hot stock and stir briskly. Stir the gelatine liquid into the sauce and leave to cool.

Next prepare the aspic. Heat 300ml/½pt of the remaining stock and pour 2 tbsp into a cup. Sprinkle over the gelatine and stir briskly. Pour the gelatine liquid back into the hot stock and leave to cool.

Remove the chicken from the fridge and place it on a wire rack over a container to catch any drips. Whisk the sauce and ladle it carefully over the chicken to cover it with a thin, even layer. Repeat the procedure twice more, at 10-minute intervals. Cut small shapes from the vegetables and arrange them on the surface of the sauce-coated chicken.

Set the meat on a wire cake rack set over a container that is large enough to catch the drips and carefully coat the food with the aspic. Use a tablespoon to pour on a thin layer, keeping it close to the food as you work so that you can control the flow of the liquid more easily. Leave to set.

Alternatively, garnish only with a simple pattern of a fan of tarragon leaves, coating once or twice more with the aspic at 10-minute intervals if you wish.

CURLED SALMON WITH DECORATIVE VEGETABLES

Allow 225g/8oz per person (a 2.25kg/ 5lb salmon will serve 10)

INGREDIENTS
1 fresh salmon

COURT BOUILLON
2.25l/4pt water
3 medium onions, peeled
3 large carrots, peeled and sliced
3 sticks celery
3 bay leaves
6 peppercorns
small handful herbs, including parsley and thyme
300ml/½pt dry white wine

DECORATION
2 fresh, firm cucumbers

ASPIC
juice of 1 lemon
25g/1oz powdered gelatine

The sight of a whole poached salmon sitting in the centre of a buffet table is like seeing a star performer holding centre stage. It is always an impressive and appealing sight, whether it is for a celebration party or a special luncheon. For a change, try cooking the salmon covered with bouillon as it is curled around the base of a large saucepan so that the body forms this lovely, curved shape when it is cold. The finished dish takes some time to prepare, so you may find it easier to spread the preparation over two days, the first spent in poaching and skinning the salmon and the second in adding the aspic garnish.

Ask the fishmonger to clean the salmon for you, leaving the head and tail intact. When you get it home, wash the fish under cold running water and use a pointed knife or small stiff brush to remove any blood along the backbone. Use sharp scissors to cut an inverted V-shape into the tail.

Make the court bouillon by adding all the ingredients (except the wine) to a saucepan. Bring to the boil and simmer for 30 minutes. Leave to cool.

Screw up several pieces of kitchen paper to pad the inside of the fish and return it to its natural shape before it was gutted. Place the fish belly-side down in a large saucepan (about 36cm/14in wide) so that it is curved into a half-moon shape around the inside of the pan. Weigh the fish down with a bowl to prevent it rising above the liquid as it cooks. Cover the fish with the cold bouillon and the wine and bring the liquid to simmering point. Leave to simmer for 5 minutes, remove from the heat and place a tight-fitting lid on the saucepan. The fish will continue to cook while the liquid cools.

Carefully remove the curved fish to a wire cooling rack. Use a sharp knife or scissors to cut off the fins and gills and to snip the skin along the back and behind the gills and the skin around the line of the tail. Starting from the gill, scrape and peel away the skin, working with the grain of the fish, and discard it. Gently scrape away the fat (the greyish bits of flesh) but leave in the backbone and also the paper padding, which will not be visible when you cut open the fish. Cover the fish with plastic film and leave to chill in the fridge for 1 hour or until the next day if you prefer.

Prepare the aspic by boiling 1.2l/2pt of the bouillon vigorously to reduce it to 600ml/1pt. Heat the lemon juice in a bowl, sprinkle over the gelatine and briskly stir. When it has dissolved, stir the gelatine liquid into the hot bouillon, and leave to simmer, stirring continuously, for 1–2 minutes. Set to one side at room temperature.

Cut the cucumbers in half lengthwise. Use a mandolin or sharp knife to cut very thin semicircles and place them into cold salted water for 30 minutes. Rinse in a sieve under cold running water and leave to dry on clean kitchen towel. Working from the tail, lay the cucumber semicircles in rows, so that the straight side is hidden under the row above. Cover the whole body with cucumber pieces to create a scale-like pattern. Add more cucumber decorations to simulate the fins. For a simpler pattern, overlap whole slices of cucumber to represent scales.

If you wish, garnish the salmon with small vegetable decorations – make a creeping stem of flowers along the side or create a more abstract pattern with tear-drop and diamond-shaped pieces of vegetables.

When you are satisfied with the decoration, chill the fish while you prepare the aspic. Pour the liquid aspic into a small bowl and place this bowl in a large bowl containing ice cubes and chilled water. Stir the aspic until it begins to thicken, and as soon as it achieves the consistency of thick oil, place the salmon on a rack and spoon over it a layer of aspic. If the aspic becomes too thick before you have coated the fish, remelt it gently over warm water, collecting any that has dripped through the rack. Chill it over chilled water as necessary.

GRAVLAX SHELL MOULD

SERVES 6
EQUIPMENT
1 tin shell mould or ring mould to hold
600ml/1pt

INGREDIENTS
GRAVLAX MOUSSE
350g/12oz salmon gravlax, diced
2 tbsp mustard sauce
5 tbsp soured cream
1½ tsp powdered gelatine
2 tbsp light fish stock or water
16 long chives for garnish

MUSTARD SAUCE
4 tbsp Dijon mustard
40g/1½oz caster sugar
5 tbsp sunflower oil
1 tbsp distilled malt vinegar
1 tbsp dill, finely chopped

Gravlax, a great delicacy in Scandinavia, is pickled salmon, and it is traditionally eaten with piquant mustard and dill sauce. You can prepare gravlax yourself or buy it, often complete with its delicious sauce, from many supermarkets and fishmongers. It looks especially attractive moulded as a mousse into a shell shape and decorated with fresh chives. A simple recipe for the mustard sauce is also included, in case you cannot buy it with the pickled salmon. The sauce also makes a delicious accompaniment to hard-boiled gulls' eggs when they are in season. For a starter for four people you will need 12 gulls' eggs. These are usually sold ready cooked, but if you need to prepare them yourself they will need 10 minutes in boiling water (see also pages 56–57). Serve the gulls' eggs or the gravlax mousse with mustard sauce spooned into small natural shells with a side plate of brown bread and butter.

Place the fish, mustard sauce and soured cream in a food processor and blend. Sprinkle the gelatine over the fish stock or water and leave for several minutes before dissolving over hot water. Allow to cool for about 10 minutes before stirring quickly into the mousse.

Rinse the mould with cold water and shake off the excess liquid. Carefully spread the gravlax mixture into the mould, making sure you fill all the corners; don't worry if it does not quite reach the top of the mould. Smooth the surface with a spatula, then leave in the refrigerator for at least 5 hours.

Before serving, dip the mould briefly into hot water and place a round plate over the mould. A sharp shake should loosen the mousse, which will come out with a slight squelch. Repeat the process if it does not come out the first time. Carefully lift away the mould and return the mousse to the fridge.

Prepare the sauce by mixing together the mustard and sugar. Then gradually whisk in the oil until the mixture is smooth and creamy. Add the vinegar and continue to whisk. Stir in the dill. Leave in the fridge until required.

Make the decorations for the mousse by dropping 16 long chives in a pan of hot water for less than 30 seconds. Drain them on kitchen paper, then use a pointed knife to arrange the chives so that they outline the mould and emphasize the ribs of the shell.

HERBS AND FLOWERS

The sweet, seductive scent of lavender evokes memories of country gardens in summer, while the warm menthol fragrance of crushed mint leaves titillates our taste buds with the pleasant anticipation of succulent roast lamb. I use my own small herb garden constantly. It is close to my kitchen door so that whatever the weather I can step outside to pick a small bouquet for garden-fresh flavourings and garnishes. I even have a mental plan of what grows where in case I need to make a night-time raid to grab a handful of leaves for a last-minute garnish during an impromptu dinner party. Having the herb garden close at hand also makes it easier for me to experiment with different flavourings and garnishes for both sweet and savoury dishes.

In general I have found that, with the exception of bay leaves, fresh herbs are best added towards the end of the cooking. A lengthy cooking seems to soak away much more of the flavour than adding them for the last 5–10 minutes. One way of overcoming this is to add the herbs or bouquet garni during cooking and then to lay a few fresh herbs on the top of the juices of a casserole to add zest to the flavour and produce a wonderful aroma as you serve the dish to your guests.

Whenever possible use young, fresh leaves because herb leaves tend to get bitter and coarse as they age. Do not use too many herbs in a single dish or you will have a confusion of tastes. Usually the strong character of one with the background flavour of a smaller amount of a second herb is sufficient.

A CORNUCOPIA OF GARNISHES
The herb garnishes illustrated opposite run, from top left to bottom right, in the order of the descriptions that follow. All the classic partners are here, including mint for lamb and sage for pork, together with some less well-known combinations.

Fish
Fennel and parsley are perfect accompaniments. Dill gives the traditional flavouring to salmon gravlax sauce, and its attractive light, feathery fronds make the ideal garnish to most delicately cooked fish dishes.

Pork
Use sweet-tasting marjoram and all varieties of sage, but for a delightful colour contrast try purple sage, which has a small, densely purple leaf. Add sprigs of the rich purple leaves around a golden roasted pork joint to make a perfect colour combination.

Poultry
Tarragon, lemon thyme and the classic sage for chicken and goose stuffing cannot be improved upon.

Lamb
The traditional trimmings of rosemary and mint are still the best.

Beef
For a change, try caraway, thyme, winter savory and myrtle. (Myrtle is also good with game.)

Game
Garden thyme imparts both flavour and a wonderfully sweet, aromatic fragrance.

Grilled Kebabs
Greek oregano, caraway, thyme and the different kinds of savory are perfect.

Tomatoes
Basil adds the most delicious tang to baked and salad tomatoes, and also to

aubergine and peppers. The fresh, bright green oval leaves are a lovely accompaniment to tomato-based pizzas and pasta. The leaves are delicate and easily bruised, so handle them gently.

New Potatoes

Add 3–4 sprigs of garden mint to 450kg/1lb of potatoes, then steam more sprigs above the water at the end of cooking for the aroma. Try spearmint, which is especially good with young potatoes and peas. Emulsify freshly cooked potatoes with melted butter and freshly snipped chive leaves, and use the tiny florets for their beautiful purple flowerheads in season.

Carrots

Rosemary or caraway make a pleasantly scented and well-flavoured change from the usual standby, parsley.

Peas

Sorrel has a slightly lemony flavour and gives a sharp, clean taste. Slightly larger quantities of sorrel will counteract the rather bland sweetness of Pea Soup (see page 44). Always use French sorrel if you can: it has a better flavour and the leaves are a prettier shape than the broad-leaved variety.

Stewed Fruits

One of the most useful herbs is sweet cicely, which has fern-like leaves and which reduces acidity. Its natural sweetness makes it ideal for dieters: try adding 2–3 leaves to gooseberries, apples or rhubarb as you cook them. You should also try angelica, which has a sweet aniseed taste. Pretty blue borage flowers make lovely garnishes to fruit cups (see page 24).

Egg

The classic flavourings and garnishes for omelettes and scrambled eggs are chervil, chives and dill.

Cakes

Caraway seeds, collected from the caraway pod, were great favourites with Victorian cooks. For sponges try lemon verbena, pineapple sage and old-fashioned marigolds, which add a spicy flavour. Scatter them over the base of the baking tin before you add the sponge mixture and their flavour will permeate through the sponge as it cooks. Decorate with sweet-scented geranium.

Bread

Try saffron, which gives both flavour and an unusual pale yellow colour, aromatic thyme and celery-tasting lovage.

Custards

Bay leaf is a good alternative to vanilla.

Vinegars

Tarragon, rosemary, basil or thyme can be added to bottles of vinegar, which can then be left in a warm place to infuse. Strain, then add fresh herbs for decoration before corking.

Decorative and Edible Flowers

Flowering herbs and edible garden flowers are fresh and appealing decorations for both savoury and sweet dishes. Cooking and garnishing with flowers is not new. In the eighteenth century Hannah Glasse was adding 'stertion' (nasturtiums) for colour and eye appeal to potted tongue.

Roses

Small flowerheads and petals look wonderful scattered over ice-cream, summer pudding and mouth-watering syllabubs. Add them to a jar of caster sugar to give fragrance and colour to the sugar, which can then be used to make rose-scented cream jellies and cakes. Red roses usually have more scent, but cream and pale yellow can look just as pretty. See Fruit and Scented Butters and Sugar (pages 68 and 81).

Strawberry Flowers

Pick tiny branches of the alpine variety, which have small white flowers and pale cream, pippy berries, which turn scarlet. Dust with sifted icing sugar to make a delicate garnish for a host of light summer puddings.

Pink and White Geraniums

Pick single flowerheads to add a soft, fragile decoration to sweet puddings and cakes. Arrange white and salmon pink geraniums alternately with violets around the edge of a sugar-frosted cake for an appealing and unusual presentation.

Borage

Clear, cool fruit punches and summer cordials can be embellished with sprigs of the velvety, electric blue flowers and the young leaves. Float the five-pointed flowerheads on top of individual drinks or press them into the surface of soft cheeses. Old herbalists used to believe that drinks with borage were good for heart conditions and made men and women 'glad and merry'.

Chrysanthemums

The whole flowerhead is rather heavy for decorating dishes, but the petals look cool and stylish scattered over a salad, a savoury tart or some Chinese dishes, for which they are a traditional accompaniment.

Marigolds

Aptly named 'a herb of the sun' by the seventeenth-century herbalist Nicholas Culpeper, marigolds were believed to ward off all ills. Because the flowers had culinary uses as well, the plants were often called pot marigolds, and today we can add a few petals to a home-made custard to give a delicate colour and spicy flavour or sprinkle them in the traditional fashion over a Cornish leek soup called Kettle Broth. Scatter a few petals over a salad for a dazzling garnish.

Violets

The tiny flowers look pretty in salads, but they can also be candied and used to decorate syllabubs and sponge cakes.

Nasturtiums

Although they have a somewhat peppery taste, we really use them for their hot red and orange shades, which look stunning with the greens of the salad bowl. Cooler effects can be achieved by the varieties that have salmon pink or creamy lemon petals.

Thyme

The tiny flower sprigs garnish many of the dishes flavoured by this versatile and aromatic herb, from forcemeat, rabbit and hare to some vegetables.

Chives

Use small clusters of the flowerheads to decorate salads and egg and potato dishes and to garnish creamy mascarpone or goat's cheese – press them into the soft surface of the cheese.

Heartsease

These tiny, deep purple pansies look summery and delicate scattered over a simple green salad or mixed into a salad made with more brightly coloured ingredients, including perhaps other edible flowers, scarlet salad leaves or sprigs of purple sage.

Lavender

The perfect garnish for lavender sorbet and even some savoury dishes.

Clover

The soft mauve-pink heads will give a salad a pretty country-garden look.

FRESH FRUIT CUP WITH HERBS AND HERB FLOWERS

This is a refreshing, non-alcoholic drink that uses several herbs for both flavour and fragrance.

INGREDIENTS
110g/4oz caster sugar
450ml/¾pt water
juice of 2 lemons
juice of 6 oranges or 150ml/5fl oz freshly squeezed orange juice
1 large sprig each of pineapple sage, eau-de-Cologne mint and lemon verbena
8 or more strawberries, sliced
1 ripe peach or mango, sliced
1 apple, sliced
600ml/1pt ginger beer

DECORATION
sprigs of pineapple sage, eau-de-Cologne mint and lemon verbena
several sprigs of borage flowers or 6–7 freshly picked flowerheads
sprays of alpine strawberries and leaves

Place the sugar in a large bowl. Boil the water and pour it over the sugar. Add the citrus juices and herbs to the warm liquid so that their scents will be infused as it cools. Strain the liquid into a glass serving bowl and add the sliced fruit. Chill in the fridge for several hours. Before serving, pour in the ginger beer, remove the herbs and refresh with sprigs of fresh herbs and borage flowers.

MANDARIN AND ROSEMARY
FLOWER JELLIES

MAKES 4 SMALL JELLIES

INGREDIENTS
*450ml/¾pt freshly squeezed mandarin
juice
zest of 3 mandarins
strip of lemon zest, about 7.5cm/3in long
150ml/5fl oz water
110g/4oz sugar
5–6 sprigs rosemary, about 5cm/2in long,
roughly bruised with a knife
12g/½oz powdered gelatine*

The bright tangy yellow of the jelly is a stunning contrast with the yellow nasturtiums that I picked in my garden. Cream flavoured with cointreau is the perfect partner for the delicate combined flavours of mandarin and rosemary. Buy ready-squeezed fresh mandarin juice, which is available in most supermarkets, to save on elbow grease. Simply double the quantities to make enough for second helpings.

Make the jelly by placing all the ingredients, except the gelatine, in a saucepan and bring slowly to the boil, stirring continuously. pour about 3 tbsp of the hot liquid from the pan into a cup and sprinkle over the powdered gelatine. Stir briskly with a fork until the gelatine looks dissolved, then turn down the heat under the saucepan so that the liquid is simmering and pour in the gelatine. Leave on a gentle, but bare simmer for 20 minutes, then strain through a jelly bag or fine sieve lined with muslin. Pour the liquid into four small moulds and leave overnight in the fridge to set.

Turn out the jellies by dipping the outside of each mould in warm to hot water. Cover the mould with a small plate, turn upside down and shake firmly once or twice. The jelly should slip out onto the plate, but repeat the process if necessary. Serve each jelly with lightly whipped Cointreau Cream.

COINTREAU CREAM
*300ml/½pt chilled double cream
1 tbsp cointreau
1 tbsp good quality of apricot jam, sieved*

Beat all the ingredients together until soft peaks are formed. Serve straightaway.

SALADS

There is a great deal of fun to be had in creating salads with the large and varied range of beautiful and colourful ingredients available today. The sheer variety can, however, be somewhat misleading, and our salads are in danger of becoming rather unhappy combinations of colours and textures that confuse both the eye and the taste buds. With the importance of colour and flavour in mind, I have designed two basic salads, to which you can – cautiously – add or subtract according to the availability of the ingredients. First, however, some do's and don't's.

Avoid sliced hard-boiled eggs, especially if they are still warm, because they usually look messy. Instead, use tiny hard-boiled quails' eggs, which look much prettier, especially if you leave on a few of their speckled shells and decorate them with fresh chives.

Think small, especially when it comes to potatoes and tomatoes. Use small sweet cherry tomatoes instead of slices of large tomatoes, and small, waxy new potatoes look better than sliced or diced large ones.

For a good combination of taste and colour, mix more strongly flavoured leaves such as radicchio, rocket, red oak

and lamb's lettuce with about twice as much of a milder leaf, such as frisée iceberg or a delicious garden-fresh green lettuce, and whenever possible use garden-fresh ingredients. Even if you have only a few fresh leaves, their fragrance will make the simplest salad more memorable.

Do not add vinaigrette to a salad too long before serving. It is better to pour the vinaigrette into the bottom of the bowl, place the crossed serving spoons over the vinaigrette and to lay the leaves over the spoons so that the salad stays crisp until the last moment, when it can be mixed at table.

For a cool-looking salad choose leaves of contrasting shapes and shades

of green. The long, jagged leaves of dandelion and rocket (which is said to have a flavour midway between mangetout peas and cress) are a perfect contrast to the light, crinkled leaves of curly endive and the sturdier, sweeter tasting leaves of cos, which is always a good standby when you want a fresh taste, crunch and bulk in a salad. Herb leaves bring taste and colour: try salad burnet, borage leaves, with their slight hint of cucumber, or purple basil. Finally, add a touch of French sorrel and garnish with a few flowerheads, such as dainty heartsease.

A hot-coloured salad can be made from a base of crisp garden lettuce, to give crunch and bulk, with a few beautiful scarlet radicchio leaves. Flavour with some lightly chopped basil leaves and garnish with a sprig of golden marjoram. Chive leaves give a good oniony flavour and can be used instead of spring onions. Chopped parsley or dill (which tastes a little like parsley) and the bright heads of nasturtiums and old-fashioned marigolds add pepperiness and colour, while deep-fried julienne of root vegetables make a crisp garnish (see pages 50 and 52).

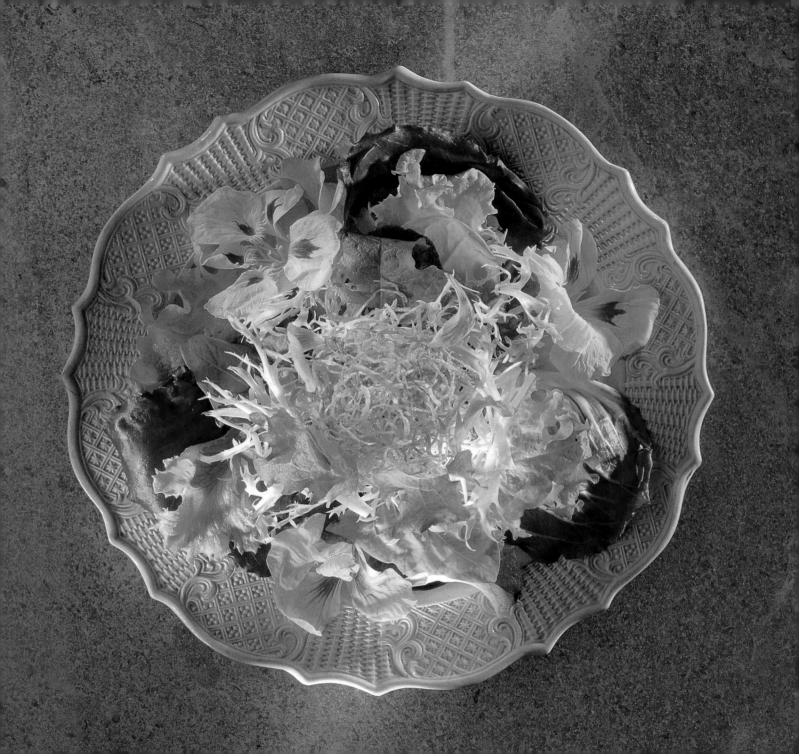

SALAD DRESSINGS

There are so many different dressings and vinaigrettes and so many flavoured oils and vinegars available today that there is almost no limit on the flavours we can bring to a simple salad dressing. One keen beetroot grower always uses the ruby red pickling juices in his vinaigrette, and this always seems to taste delicious with his chosen salad ingredients. I often use the thin, watered-down vinaigrette from the previous day's salad bowl as a stock for vegetarian dishes. Fruit vinaigrette is a good accompaniment for summer salads, and it can be easily made from the juices left in a large bowl of fresh fruit salad combined with wine vinegar.

When time is short, it is always useful to have a quick reference of the vinaigrettes that can be used with different dishes, and some of my own favourites are listed here. The split port vinaigrette always looks impressive, and, as the name suggests, the oil and wine reduction separate to give a beautifully mottled, bubbly effect. Add garlic and herbs whenever you think they will be appropriate. The emulsions may separate if they are left to stand but will return to their former glory with a whisk before serving.

BASIC VINAIGRETTE

INGREDIENTS
2 tsp Dijon mustard
4 tsp white wine vinegar
300ml/½pt vegetable oil
a little water to adjust consistency
seasoning to taste

Whisk the ingredients together in a bowl and add the seasoning.

Pommery
Follow the recipe for basic vinaigrette, but use Pommery mustard instead of Dijon mustard. This dressing goes well with chicken and turbot.

Tomato
Whisk 1 tsp tomato purée into the basic recipe, then add 65g/2½oz diced concasse for a delicious accompaniment to vegetarian, asparagus and seafood dishes.

Saffron
Infuse a good pinch of saffron strands or powdered saffron in 1 tbsp hot water and add to the basic recipe. Use with shellfish and fish dishes, especially poached salmon.

STRAWBERRY VINAIGRETTE

INGREDIENTS
4 tbsp salad oil
1 tbsp lemon juice
4 large fresh strawberries
caster sugar to taste
salt and freshly ground pepper

Place the oil, juice and strawberries in a blender and mix until smooth. Add sugar and seasoning to taste.

BALSAMIC VINAIGRETTE

This is the ideal dressing for salads accompanying poultry, beef or fish.

INGREDIENTS
2 tsp Dijon mustard
4 tsp balsamic vinegar
2 tsp soft brown sugar
½ tsp tomato purée
150ml/5fl oz vegetable oil
150ml/5fl oz olive oil
seasoning to taste
a little water to adjust consistency

Place the mustard, vinegar, sugar and tomato purée in a bowl and whisk together thoroughly. Slowly add the

vegetable oil, followed by the olive oil. Season to taste and add a little water to thin down if necessary.

Split Port Vinaigrette

Use this with salads served with pigeon, venison and most game dishes.

INGREDIENTS
150ml/5fl oz ruby red port
150ml/5fl oz red wine
25g/1oz brown sugar
30ml/2 tbsp red wine vinegar
30ml/2 tbsp vegetable oil
30ml/2 tbsp olive oil

Add the port, red wine and sugar to a saucepan and reduce over a moderate heat to 30ml/2tbsp of liquid. Add the reduction to a mixing bowl and whisk in the remaining ingredients. Mix again thoroughly just before using.

Cliff's Beetroot Dressing
Add some of the ruby red juices from home-cooked beetroot steeped in vinegar and sugar to the basic vinaigrette recipe and whisk. This is delicious with a garden-fresh salad of cos lettuce, spring onions and cherry tomatoes, hard-boiled eggs and new, waxy potatoes in butter and mint.

Fruit Salad Bowl Vinaigrette
Combine the sweet, fruity juices left over from a large bowl of fresh fruit salad with enough wine vinegar to sharpen the flavour – or to your taste. Season and serve with fresh summer salads containing avocado.

Basil Oil
In Italy basil is considered to be the most important of the aromatic herbs. It has a distinctive, tangy flavour, which can enliven the simplest of tomato sauces or salad dressings. Sadly for most of us, it flourishes only in summer, but you can try to preserve it fragrance all year round by adding a large bunch of fresh leaves to a bottle of extra virgin olive oil (about 600ml/1pt). To encourage the spiciness of the leaves to permeate the oil, leave the bottle on a sunny windowsill or in a greenhouse for several weeks, shaking it occasionally. Strain into a clean bottle and add a few fresh leaves before using for frying tomatoes, peppers and aubergines. Alternatively, mix the flavoured oil with garlic paste, which you can make by creaming the flesh of a garlic with 1 tsp salt, and stir into freshly cooked pasta or drizzle over a salad of beefsteak tomatoes.

SEAFOOD WITH MARINATED SWEET PEPPER SALAD

SERVES 4

INGREDIENTS
3 large red capsicum peppers
1 large yellow capsicum pepper

SWEET PEPPER MARINADE
4 tbsp extra virgin olive oil
4 tbsp walnut oil
2 tbsp balsamic vinegar
½ tsp sweet chili sauce
1 rounded dssp chopped parsley
ground sea salt and black pepper to taste

SALAD
1 small aubergine, sliced, or several Chinese aubergines, halved
1–2 tbsp olive oil
1 large courgette, sliced into 5mm/¼in ovals
8 or more large Pacific prawns
4 green lettuce leaves, such as frisée or lollo biondi
4 red lettuce leaves, such as radicchio, oak leaf or lollo rosso
4 sprigs of basil leaves to garnish

Fish-shaped plates are perfect for serving seafood. Look out for them in antique markets, where they often turn up in sets. The styles vary enormously – from 1950s kitsch to more valuable nineteenth-century majolica. I like to mop up the last juices with home-made bread, such as Wild Garlic or Onion Focaccia, or Pugliese, a wonderful bread made with semolina, or the delicious bread rolls on page 64.

Slice each pepper lengthways into four and scrape out and discard the white ribs and seeds. Set the peppers, skin side down, on a lightly oiled baking sheet in a preheated oven at 220°C/ 425°F/gas mark 7 for 25 minutes until the skins look blistered and charred. Take the peppers from the oven and leave them, wrapped tightly in a plastic bag, until they are cool, when the skins will peel from the flesh quite easily. Cut into strips 2.5cm/1in wide.

Whisk together the ingredients for the marinade and pour the mix over the pepper strips. Leave to one side.

Salt the aubergine and dry the pieces on kitchen paper to remove the bitter juices. Sauté in oil with the courgettes until they are crisply golden but still al dente. Arrange the aubergines and courgettes on serving plates with the prawns, salad leaves and strips of pepper.

Drain the remaining marinade back into a small saucepan and set over a low heat to warm before drizzling it over the salad. Garnish with basil leaves and serve immediately.

BALLOTTINE OF CORN-FED CHICKEN WITH PISTACHIO NUTS AND HERBS

This delicious dish comes from Alan Ford, the head chef of Hintlesham Hall, one of Suffolk's most respected restaurants. The chicken is boned and re-formed around a rich pistachio mousse mixture, which is further enriched with madeira and cooked in a water bath set in the oven. It is visually very attractive and can be prepared in advance, with just the salad left to the day of the meal. The arrangement of the sliced ballottine with a central core of mixed, dressed salad makes a simple yet striking dish.

SERVES 4

INGREDIENTS
4 breasts of corn-fed chicken
good pinch of salt
1–2 tbsp madeira
300ml/½pt double cream
55g/2oz blanched and peeled pistachio nuts
1 tbsp chopped, mixed fresh herbs
salt and pepper
balsamic vinaigrette (see page 30)

BALLOTTINE
6 breasts of corn-fed chicken
salt and freshly ground pepper
12 large leaves of spinach, blanched

Begin by making the mousse filling. Remove the skin and bones from the chicken breasts and cut the meat into small cubes. Process in a food processor until smooth, then press the meat through a fine sieve to remove remaining fibres. (This last stage is not essential but improves the appearance of the finished dish.) Return to the goblet and chill for 20 minutes. Add the salt and madeira to the goblet and blend. Add the cream slowly and continue to blend until it is incorporated. Do not overbeat or the mixture may separate. Turn the mixture into a bowl, stir in the nuts and herbs and season to taste.

Assemble the ballottine by skinning the six breasts and beating them, one at a time, between pieces of kitchen film until they are twice the original size. Lay a piece of kitchen film measuring 43 x 23cm/17 x 9in on your work surface and place on it the six breasts, skin side down, so that they cover about two-thirds of the area of the film. Season with salt and pepper. Dry the blanched spinach leaves in kitchen paper and place them over the chicken breasts. Spoon the mousse down the centre to form a roll about 4cm/1½in

thick. Pull one side of the kitchen film over towards the other side to form the chicken into a sausage shape, and twist the ends of the film together, tying them with string for extra security. Wrap the sausage tightly in kitchen foil. Cook in a baking tray half-filled with water at 190°C/375°F/gas mark 5 for about 30 minutes. Test if it is cooked by piercing the centre with a fine needle. When the tip of the needle is hot, the ballottine is cooked. Remove from the water and leave to cool.

Chill in the fridge for at least 4 hours so that it becomes firm. Remove the foil and film and, holding your knife at a slight angle, cut slices about 1cm/½in thick. Allow the ballottine to stand at room temperature for 15–20 minutes because the texture of the mousse and chicken will be too firm and over-chilled if you serve it straight from the fridge. Arrange three or four medallions around the edge of each plate, and serve with a small salad of mixed leaves in the centre. Drizzle over the balsamic vinaigrette.

VEGETABLES

There are few more delicious treats than young, freshly cooked vegetables: pencil-slim carrots, as small as a finger and with a feathery green leaf top-knot; new potatoes, some as small as broad beans, with a rich, earthy smell and skins so delicate you can rub them away with a finger nail; french beans straight from the garden; courgettes, their pretty yellow flowers still attached, which are so prized by restaurateurs; and peas, almost too good to put into the saucepan as you press open each pod. These vegetables need no added flavourings or garnishes except a soupçon of butter to enrich and glaze them after cooking.

Even if you don't have a garden of your own, don't worry. Make friends with a keen gardener and exchange their fresh produce for your home-made cakes and pies! A more realistic solution, perhaps, is to go to a vegetable market or a produce stall of the kind run in England and Wales by the Women's Institute. These stalls generally groan under freshly dug and harvested produce from local gardens and small-holdings, and it is often the case that some of the more unusual vegetables like rhubarb chard, yellow courgettes and purple-podded beans are less keenly sought after and are the last to go.

These days supermarkets stock huge ranges of fresh and flavoursome young vegetables, although it would be more interesting if the produce wasn't so carefully trimmed and tidied. Then we could serve root vegetables with tiny green feathers on top or courgettes with flowers and smell the scents of the garden as we scrubbed the earth from unwashed potatoes.

COOKING YOUNG VEGETABLES
Young vegetables should be cooked differently from, and more quickly than, their older counterparts. This method retains both their delicate appearance and the flavour.

Vegetables fall into two main groups when it comes to cooking – hard and soft. Hard vegetables include carrots, baby navets (turnips) and baby sweetcorn. Soft vegetables, which take less time to cook, include mangetout peas, asparagus and french beans.

To cook 450g/1lb of hard vegetables, trim if necessary but keep them whole. Plunge them into a large saucepan containing 2.25l/4pt of well-salted, rapidly boiling water, and cook them, uncovered, for 3 minutes. Drain and refresh in a bowl of cold water until cold. Drain again and store, covered, in the refrigerator. Just before serving place 25g/1oz of butter and 4 tbsp of water in a medium sized saucepan and bring to a hard boil. Add the vegetables and salt and pepper, cover with a lid or buttered paper and leave to boil for 1 minute, then cook uncovered for a further minute (although this will depend on the size of the vegetable). They are ready when tender to the tip of a knife.

MEDLEY OF MIXED VEGETABLES
To cook a mixture of soft and hard vegetables, such as carrots, turnips, baby sweetcorn, asparagus, mangetout peas and french beans with a total weight of 450g/1lb, first cook the hard vegetables as above for 3 minutes. The carrots, turnips and sweetcorn should be cooked in separate pans in 1l/2pt of water. Strain and drop them into cold water.

Meanwhile, cook the peas, beans and asparagus separately for 1 minute in boiling salted water. Strain and add to the cold water with the other vegetables. Strain the vegetables together and tip into one bowl. Cover with kitchen film and place in the refrigerator.

To reheat, add the butter and water to a medium sized saucepan and bring to a fast boil before adding the vegetables. Cook covered for 1 minute, then uncovered for a further minute. Add a soupçon of extra butter if you wish. Strain and serve hot.

SERVING VEGETABLES

Pile a spoonful of peas onto a small, dark green chard leaf. The dark green will be the perfect foil to the perfect, pale green peas.

Add a generous sprinkling of finely snipped chives and melted butter to new potatoes.

Try a dash of red to add zing to a plate of all-green vegetables. Rhubarb chard, another member of the chard family, has wonderful wine red veins in its deep green leaves, or try small, immature baby beetroots, a small tuft of leaves still attached at the top. If you grow your own courgettes (or have friends who do) always leave the glorious yellow flowers trailing from one or two of the vegetables to create a beautiful, natural looking arrangement.

POTATOES

The arrival of the potato in Europe was instrumental in bringing about the demise of the bag pudding, which had previously been the staple and filling accompaniment to meat. When potatoes were introduced into England in the reign of Elizabeth I they achieved great popularity – one contemporary banquet featured potatoes in every course.

Today there are hundreds of varieties, although supermarkets and greengrocers stock only limited ranges. It is worth making a note of the name of any varieties that you particularly like so that you can remember the ones that have the best flavour and respond best to different ways of cooking.

Basic cooking is quite simple. To boil older potatoes, cook them slowly in moderately simmering water. Young potatoes should be cooked quickly in boiling water. Test both for tenderness by inserting the point of a knife.

Mealy or floury potatoes are better for mashing than for boiling or frying. New potatoes are not good for mashing or roasting, but their firm, waxy texture and fresh, earthy taste make them ideal for salads or for teaming with thick cream and gruyère cheese in a luxurious dauphinoise.

Potatoes cut and prepared for paille and game chips should be rinsed in cold water before deep-frying to remove the starch that causes the potato straws or discs to stick together as they cook.

The opposite rule applies to potatoes prepared for dishes such as dauphinoise or Pommes Anna. Here, the peeled and cut potatoes should be used without rinsing because the starch helps the layers stick together to give the cake-like result you want.

The following recipes are sufficient for four people.

SWEET POTATOES

When they are candied or mashed with spices sweet potatoes are more often associated with the American celebration of Thanksgiving. However, their unusual flavour, not unlike that of chestnuts, makes them a perfect partner for both light coloured meats and poultry and also for some game dishes, especially rabbit.

This recipe dates from Tudor times. Peel and boil 450g/1lb sweet potatoes (they take less time to cook than ordinary potatoes). Add plenty of butter and mash finely with 1 tbsp of rosewater (optional), 1 dssp soft brown sugar, the grated rind and scant juice of half an orange, a squeeze of lemon juice and a pinch of nutmeg and salt. Bake at 180°C/350°F/gas mark 4 for 30 minutes.

SAFFRON POTATOES

I use a waxy potato for this recipe – knobbly tubers of Pink Fir Apple, for example, although any other new potato can be used. Soak a good pinch of saffron strands in 2 tbsp of warm water for 1 hour. Sauté the potatoes in 25g/1oz of butter for 2 minutes, shaking the pan to keep the potatoes moving. Add the saffron juice with a

bay leaf, a sprig of thyme and salt and freshly ground pepper. After 30 seconds, add 100ml/3½ fl oz of chicken stock, cover with buttered paper and leave to simmer for 15 minutes. Remove the paper and boil hard to reduce the remaining juices to glaze the potatoes. Serve in a nest of shiny dark green bay leaves, which contrast perfectly with the pretty yellow potatoes.

POMMES GAUFRETTES
These latticed rounds of potato are especially suitable for game dishes. Peel and slice potatoes on a mandolin using the crinkled or toothed blade. Hold a potato with the palm of your hand and cut straight down. Turn the potato through 90 degrees and cut down again over the blade to make a criss-cross pattern. If holes do not appear, the slices are too thick; if the slices look stringy, they are too thin. You will probably need to experiment before you get the right thickness. Deep-fry until golden.

POTATO STRAWS OR POMMES PAILLES
You need a sharp knife to cut these extra-fine chips. Cut and shape 2–3 large potatoes into long, evenly sized oblongs, 5mm/¼in or less thick. Hold the shapes stacked together in one hand and work them over the plain blade of a mandolin to create matchsticks. Deep fry at 195°C/385°F until they are crisp and pale golden. Drain and serve

immediately, because they tend to soften almost as soon as they have been cooked.

POTATO STRAW CAKES OR GALETTES
Use medium sized peeled potatoes and julienne them. Add 2 tbsp of clarified butter to a frying pan that is large enough to accommodate four round tin pastry cutters, each 9–9.5cm/3½–3¾in across. Place the pastry cutters in the pan and set the pan over a low to moderate heat. When the fat is hot add about 55g/2oz of strips so that they fit neatly inside each pastry cutter. Use a palette knife or small spatula to press the strips firmly inside the moulds as they cook. Use an oven glove or tea towel to hold the tin cutters in place. Sauté for 5–6 minutes, when the top of the potatoes will begin to look soft and mould into the circles.

Remove the moulds and carefully turn over each of the galettes with a wide spatula. Reduce the cooking temperature and cook for a further 7–8 minutes until soft right through to the point of a knife. Serve immediately or leave in a low oven briefly to keep warm.

POMMES PARISIENNES
Peel 4 large potatoes and use a round melon-ball cutter to scoop out the flesh, pressing the tool down into the potato and twisting it around to remove small balls. Keep the potatoes in water to prevent discoloration until you need them, then cook in boiling water for

2 minutes. Drain thoroughly on kitchen paper. Melt equal amounts of butter and oil in a large frying pan set over high heat and add the potato balls. Reduce the temperature after 30 seconds and leave to simmer, turning frequently in the hot fat until the balls are crisp and golden. Drain and keep warm, covered in foil, until just before serving.

TURNED AND RIBBED POTATOES
This is an ideal way to use old potatoes with a traditional roast. Use a sharp knife to cut medium sized potatoes into pieces that are more or less the same size and trim them into ovals. Evenly sized potatoes always look better when you come to serve them. Cook the potatoes in simmering water for 5 minutes until they are tender, then drain and leave to cool. Cut into slices, leaving a thin, uncut rib of flesh at the base of each potato so that the discs do not separate. Add to the roasting pan with hot dripping and bake at 220°C/425°F/gas mark 7 for 30 minutes. Baste well and cook for a further 15 minutes until golden brown.

PETITES POMMES ANNA
You will need four small round baking tins, each about 10cm/4in across, in addition to 900g/2lb of new or old potatoes no longer than 5cm/2in long, 55g/2oz of butter at room temperature. Soften the butter with a knife and divide it into four. Peel the potatoes and cut or slice them on a mandolin

into thin rounds. Dry them in a clean tea towel but do not store them in water because they will lose their starch, which holds them together and gives the liquid in which they are cooked a creamy consistency. Rub the inside of the baking tins with half the butter and arrange inside each two overlapping circles of potato slices. Lay the first circle overlapping in one direction and the second circle overlapping in the opposite direction. Add small dabs of butter to the layers, making sure that you do not disturb the potato slices, and season well. Arrange more overlapping potatoes, adding dabs of butter between layers, although these rows need not be so neatly arranged. You should have four layers in each baking tin. Finally, press a ring of buttered paper over each filled tin and use a double thickness of close-fitting kitchen foil to cover each one. Cook slowly on a hot plate for 6 minutes, then finish off in the oven for a further 10 minutes or until the potatoes seem soft when tested with a pointed knife. Keep warm for a short time. Alternatively, turn out the pretty shapes when the tins are cool enough to handle and microwave for 1 minute on high just before serving.

The Perfect Mash

The French have a great liking for puréed potatoes prepared in a mouli. These potatoes have a soft, velvety texture, which always looks better when you serve them, and they are ideal for piping into shapes around a dish such as Coquilles St Jacques or for duchess potatoes

Cook 900g/2lb of potatoes until they are soft, drain and place them on a low heat covered with a tea towel to allow the excess moisture to evaporate. Pass through a mouli, then beat in several knobs of butter, a pinch of nutmeg or mace, a squeeze of garlic juice (optional) and enough hot milk or cream to cream the mixture. Finally, correct the seasoning with salt and ground black pepper.

For a change, try adding a cooked, puréed apple to the mash when you are serving it with liver and bacon or something similar. The addition of a small amount of mashed swede or sweet potato will give a pleasing and distinctive flavour, which will go well with poultry and pork. Mashed celeriac tastes particularly good when it is combined with potatoes and garlic juice as an accompaniment for game dishes.

Pomme Fritte Basket

These are the ideal holders for sautéed potatoes or Pommes Parisiennes or any other small, cooked vegetables such as broad beans in creamy chervil sauce or minted garden pea.

Equipment
1 metal nest-maker or 2 small, long-handled wire sieves that will fit one inside the other

Makes 4

Ingredients
2 large, long potatoes
oil for deep-frying

Peel the potatoes but do not rinse them in water because the starch helps to stick the pieces together while they cook. Slice the potatoes very thinly lengthways, using a mandolin if you have one, then slice the oval discs into long, thin matchstick-like pieces. Divide the matchsticks into four separate piles.

Briefly dip the hinged nest-maker into hot oil and shake off the excess. This helps prevent the potato strips from sticking to it as they are deep-fried. Spread potato sticks around the inside of the larger nest so that they resemble a nest and place the smaller basket on the top of the potato. Hold the two baskets together by means of the handles. Deep-fry in very hot oil for about 2 minutes or until the potato strips are mid-gold in colour. The base of the nest will need an extra 30 seconds, and you will need to hold the top half of the nest above the surface of the oil while the base is allowed to cook for a little longer.

Gently ease the nest from the basket, using a palette knife if necessary, then leave to drain and cool, turned upside down on kitchen paper or over up-turned cups covered in kitchen paper. The nests can be reheated in a low oven if necessary.

PEA SOUP

Allow 1.35kg/3lb of pea pods to give 450g/1lb shelled peas

INGREDIENTS
55g/2oz butter
1 medium onion, chopped
1 clove garlic, crushed
1 whole, crisp, green garden lettuce, washed and dried
sprig of tarragon, snipped
3 sprigs of parsley, snipped
7–8 sorrel leaves
450g/1lb podded peas
850ml/1½pt chicken stock
2 tbsp double cream
salt and freshly ground pepper

THOMAS LAXTON
GARDEN PEAS

The beams of June sunlight pick out a plate of bright green peapods and sorrel leaves and catch reflections from a glass soup bowl, filled with a delicately coloured, delicious soup, garnished with a single pea flower. The slightly bitter tasting sorrel leaves are an essential counterbalance to the sweetness of the peas. If you do not grow your own, look out for sorrel in local herb gardens and choose French sorrel, which has a better flavour and prettier leaves than broad-leaved sorrel.

Heat the butter in a pan and slowly sweat the onion and garlic until they are pale gold. Stir in the lettuce leaves and herbs and cook for a further minute. Transfer to a larger pan and add the peas and the stock. Bring to the boil and simmer for 4–5 minutes until the peas are tender. Take care not to overcook them. Purée and sieve the soup back into the pan, then stir in the cream. Slowly reheat and season to taste before serving.

HOW TO COOK AND PRESENT YOUNG PEAS

Allow 225g/8oz per person, before shelling

Shell the peas and put them, with a sprig of mint leaves, into a medium sized saucepan of salted, boiling water. Leave to cook on a steady boil for about 5 minutes or until tender – older peas will take longer – then strain off the pale green liquor. Tip the hot peas into a heated tureen and stir in a large knob of butter and several whole peapods for garnish.

For a pretty summer presentation, place the bowl of hot peas inside a serving basket decorated with freshly picked sprigs of pea flowers and leaves and some flowering herbs.

TWO POTATO GRATINS

The next two potato recipes are very similar, but the potatoes are cut in different ways. In one of the recipes the potatoes are finely shredded into straws; in the other the potatoes are cut into thin discs. Both are baked and grilled gratin-style to give an appealing and appetizing thin brown crust.

BAKED STRAW POTATOES

The anchovies, which add a mild but more-ish flavour, should be soaked in milk before you begin.

EQUIPMENT
1 round or oval enamelled gratin dish

SERVES 4

INGREDIENTS
55g/2oz anchovies, soaked in milk
1 small onion (80–110g/3–4oz)
800g/1¾lb potatoes
butter
ground black pepper
350ml/12fl oz single cream

Drain the anchovies and chop them finely. Slice the onion finely and cut the potato into long, thin strips on a mandolin. Butter the gratin dish generously and lay the potatoes, onion and anchovies in alternate layers, ending with a layer of potatoes. Season each layer with a little pepper. Do not add salt because anchovies are already salty. Pour over the cream and bake for 20 minutes at 200°C/400°F/gas mark 6; lower the temperature to 190°C/375°F/gas mark 5 and cook for a further 15 minutes. Set under a hot grill for 1 minute to finish. Paint the surface lightly with a little hot clarified butter before serving.

POTATO DAUPHINOISE

The taste and texture of this dish will improve, and it will be easier to slice, if it is made the day before.

EQUIPMENT
1 round or oval enamelled gratin dish

SERVES 4

INGREDIENTS
1 small garlic clove
55g/2oz butter
800g/1¾lb waxy new potatoes, scrubbed
300ml/½ pt milk
several sprigs of thyme and parsley, chopped
1 small onion, peeled and thinly sliced
salt and freshly ground black pepper
25g/1oz gruyère cheese, grated
150ml/5fl oz double cream

Peel and bruise the garlic clove in salt, then rub the juices over the inside of the dish with about 12g/½oz of butter. Slice the potatoes thinly, preferably on a mandolin so that the slices are more or less the same thickness. Scald the milk and remove it from the heat just before it comes to boil. Add a layer of potatoes to the dish and pour over a little milk. Add some dots of butter and continue to add alternately layers of potato, herbs and onion, pouring over milk each time. Sprinkle over the cheese before adding the last layer of potatoes, which should be arranged so that they overlap to make a neat fish-scale pattern. Dot with the remaining butter and pour over the cream. Cover with a lid of parchment, pressed around the rim of the tin. Bake in a preheated oven at 190°C/375°F/gas mark 5 for 15 minutes, then reduce the temperature to 180°C/350°F/gas mark 4 and cook for a further 1 hour. Remove the cover and set under a hot grill to finish off.

BREAST OF PHEASANT AND OYSTER MUSHROOMS WITH PORT SAUCE

SERVES 6

INGREDIENTS
3 pheasants, prepared
900g/2lb chicken and pheasant bones
225g/8oz mirepoix of carrot, leek,
onion and celery
½ clove garlic
½ bay leaf
several sprigs thyme
1 dssp tomato purée
3 shallots, roughly chopped
150ml/5fl oz ruby port
4 shallots, sliced
110g/4oz oyster mushrooms, cut in halves
or, if very large, into quarters

This is a very rich and warming game dish, which is ideal served with deliciously prepared winter vegetables.

Divide the pheasants into portions and reserve the legs in the freezer for stews. Set the breasts to one side. Put the chicken and pheasant bones in a baking tray and cook them in a preheated oven at 190°C/375°F/gas mark 5 and roast them until they are golden-brown. Place them in a large saucepan with the mirepoix of vegetables, garlic, bay leaf, thyme and tomato purée. Pour in enough water to cover the bones and simmer gently for 3 hours, frequently skimming the surface of the stock with a slotted spoon. Strain and simmer to reduce by half. Sweat the roughly chopped shallots in a little oil for 4 minutes. Add about three-quarters of the port and reduce to 2 tbsp. Add the stock and reduce once more by about one-third. Strain and add the remaining port, then leave to simmer for a further 30–45 minutes or until the sauce looks glossy and has thickened. Roast the pheasant breasts for 15 minutes at 200°C/400°F/gas mark 6, or at a slightly higher temperature if you prefer less pink meat. Remove and wrap in foil. Leave to one side to rest. Sweat the sliced shallots in butter and add the mushrooms. Cook for 1–2 minutes or more until lightly brown. Reserve, covered in foil, in a warm oven. To serve remove the pheasant breasts from the bones and reheat them gently. Cut each one across its width into neat slices and arrange the slices in fan shapes on six plates with the shallot and mushroom mixture. Surround them with hot port sauce and serve with seasonal vegetables or mashed potatoes and pommes gaufrettes (see pages 41–2) and little cabbage parcels (see page 52).

VEGETABLES ON DISPLAY

Rather like humans, less-than-young vegetables, with their more unpredictable and fulsome shapes and more dominant flavours, can be extremely interesting. Thoughtfully treated, this older produce can look every bit as attractive and appetizing as its youthful, springtime counterparts. Complement their mature flavours by combining different shapes and colours, or cook several varieties together, making nests from julienned strips of one vegetable to hold bite-sizes pieces of another.

TURNED VEGETABLES

The word 'turning' is used to describe the sculpting of old vegetables to make them look more attractive by carving them into smaller, neater and more evenly sized shapes. This may sound like a waste of time, but they do look very elegant for a dinner party and the uniform size means that they cook evenly.

If they are still intact, trim the top-knots and tail and root ends to make them the same length. Use a small, sharp knife to shape them into similarly sized barrel or long olive shapes.

Strips of tender carrot and swede bathed in a creamy orange sauce spiked with rosemary.

SPAGHETTI VEGETABLES

These can be a colourful and pretty accompaniment to a whole range of savoury dishes. Look out in catering equipment shops for those vegetable slicing machines that can make long, spaghetti-like strands from root vegetables. These can be cooked in the same way as julienned vegetables.

JULIENNED CARROT AND SWEDE IN CREAMY ORANGE AND ROSEMARY SAUCE

The mandolin has two stainless steel blades, one crinkled one (which is useful for game chips, see page 41) and the other straight, which are set in the opposite faces of the oblong board. I find it is one of the most useful pieces of equipment in my kitchen, and here is a recipe that puts it to good use.

You will need 3 large carrots and 1 large swede. Square off the sides of the peeled carrots and swede and cut them into rectangular slices, about 3mm/⅛in thick. Stack the vegetable slices on top of each other and, holding them carefully together with your fingertips, move them over the straight blade in a strumming movement to make matchstick strips. If you do not have a mandolin, use a sharp kitchen knife to cut the thin strips. Add the vegetables to a pan of boiling salted water and cook for 1 minute. Drain well and return to the pan with 55g/2oz of butter, the juice of 1½ oranges, rosemary leaves stripped from several sprigs, 2 tsp of sugar and ½ tsp of salt. Leave to simmer gently for 1–2 minutes, turning the strips carefully

once or twice in the hot, buttery juices. Turn the vegetables into a china dish and strain the juices back into the pan. Add 2–3 tbsp cream and boil for 30 seconds until the juices have thickened. Pour over the vegetables and serve.

Alternatively, mould the vegetables into small ramekin dishes and refrigerate. De-mould onto the serving plates and microwave on medium for 1 minute until completely warmed through. Serve the little vegetable mounds decorated with tiny sprigs of rosemary or with thyme flowers when they are in season. Served with slices of cooked meat, poultry or game, arranged around the vegetables.

CUCUMBER BARRELS
Cut four 2.5cm/1in segments of cucumber. Carve out the centres, leaving 3mm/$\frac{1}{8}$in margin of flesh around the edge of the skin and a small wedge of flesh at the base to create small barrels. Plunge them into boiling, salted water for 6–7 minutes (6 minutes if you like them to have a little crunch). Drain and season with salt and pepper and serve filled with hot, buttered, minted peas.

CAULIFLOWER BUDS
Serve these with roasts and chops. Coat the buds lightly with mornay or hollandaise sauce to make them extra luxurious.

Slice leek leaves lengthways and divide them into lengths according to the size of the buds, then cut them into a point at one end. Blanch them for 3 minutes, then wrap the leaves around a steamed cauliflower or small groups of florets, with the pointed ends pressed over the top of the creamy-white heads. Serve immediately.

LITTLE CABBAGE PARCELS
Blanch 4 small, dark green cabbage leaves in boiling water for 30 seconds and drain. Chop several of the lighter green leaves from the centre of the cabbage and sauté gently in butter for about 2$\frac{1}{2}$ minutes until softened. Place small amounts of the sautéed cabbage on the whole leaves and form small, round parcels. Wrap each parcel in a piece of kitchen film and twist into a knot at the top to secure each one in a tight ball. Leave in the fridge until just before serving, when they can be reheated, still wrapped in plastic film, in boiling water for 3–4 minutes. Remove the film and serve immediately. Use to accompany Breast of Pheasant and Oyster Mushrooms with Port Sauce (see page 48).

CRISPY DEEP-FRIED ROOT VEGETABLES
Julienne some carrot and celeriac into very fine strips and deep fry them in hot oil at 160°C/320°F for about 1 minute or until the strips are a pale golden-saffron colour. Drain and serve as a lovely crunchy garnish to a salad (see page 28).

ROOT VEGETABLE GAUFRETTES
Use a mandolin to cut carrot, swede or celeriac into thin, latticed discs, following the same cutting method as for Pommes Gaufrettes (see page 41). Deep fry in hot oil at 160°C/320°F for 2–3 minutes or until crisp and golden.

GREEN BEAN NESTS
This is an ideal accompaniment for cold meat and salad dishes.

Cook the prepared beans in salted boiling water until they are tender and pliable. Drain and mould the beans around the inside and across the base of small terrine dishes. Refrigerate for 1 hour, then carefully turn out from the moulds onto serving plates. Fill with small vegetables or use them as edible containers for aioli, to serve with meat and poultry salads.

PUMPKIN SOUP

SERVES 8

INGREDIENTS
2 large onions, chopped
55g/2oz butter
2 slices bacon, cubed
1.35kg/3lb pumpkin flesh, cut into
small cubes, pith and pips removed
1.75l/3pt good chicken stock
1 large parsnip, peeled and chopped
1 large carrot, peeled and chopped
1 leek, thinly sliced
2 medium potatoes, roughly chopped
2 tomatoes, sliced
2 tbsp thick cream
salt and freshly ground black pepper

Velvety smooth, richly yellow but not tasting too overbearingly of pumpkin – more like a vegetable soup with a pronounced, sweeter fragrance and a delicious rounded flavour. If you use a large pumpkin, cut any surplus flesh (discarding pith and seeds) into cubes and freeze them for future use in soups and meat stews.

Sauté the onions until golden in the butter, then add the bacon and stir-fry for a further 1 minute. Scrape the mixture into a large saucepan, then add the remaining ingredients, except the cream.

Bring to the boil, reduce the heat and leave to simmer for about 30 minutes. Purée the cooled liquid in a blender or mouli. Reheat slowly and stir in the cream. Check the seasoning and serve piping hot in its own empty shell accompanied by chunks of oven-fresh bread and butter.

SQUASH TUREENS
Food for a Hallowe'en party, prepared on a large scale, can be served from emptied squash tureens. The vibrant orange pumpkins, grown to rival the proportions of Cinderella's coach, are ideal containers for hot golden broths, while other, smaller varieties, such as the pale cream-coloured custard marrows or the white and green stippled turban squashes – which, as their name suggests, look just like little flattened turbans – can be quickly transformed into bowls for mixed rice and salads.

MAKING A PUMPKIN SHELL TUREEN
Cut a lid carefully from the stalk end, using a sharp, long-bladed knife in a sawing, rounded, zigzag pattern as shown (left). Then carefully pull it away. Use a large spoon – and your hands – to scoop out the seeds and cottony fibres, then scrape any remaining pith away from the inside walls of the shell.

EGGS AND THE BREAKFAST TRAY

EGGS

Eggs in all their sizes, colours, flavours and shapes have been part of our diet for centuries. Eliza Acton, writing of swan's eggs in 1845, tells us: 'Only those of young birds should be used. They are more delicate than from their size might be supposed; and when boiled hard and shelled, their appearance is beautiful, the white being of remarkable purity and transparency.' In Mrs Beeton's time, swans' eggs were used for wedding cakes and grand salads.

The Chinese create what they call 'a thousand year egg', which is generally a duck egg, left coated in a clay of ashes, lime and salt for several months. This preserves the egg and colours it through the shell. When the egg is cleaned and peeled, it has solidified and become a translucent, shiny, brownish-grey-green. These eggs are considered great delicacies in China, and they are available from Chinese food stores in this country. Try them thinly sliced on rye bread as an unusual cold starter to a meal.

Then there are tea eggs, perhaps the most beautiful of all cooked eggs. Simmer finely cracked, hard-boiled eggs in spiced tea to produce a marbled pattern over the surface of the peeled egg.

Full marks for presentation go to the author of the 1868 edition of Warne's *Cookery*, who tells us that plovers' eggs, hot or cold, should be set inside small baskets covered in moss, both inside and outside, with a bent twig over the top for a handle. A similarly appealing presentation is mentioned in Evelyn Waugh's *Brideshead Revisited*: the first time Charles Ryder meets Sebastian he is 'peeling a plover's egg taken from the large nest of moss in the centre of the table'. I shall certainly try the moss

basket idea myself one day, using thin wire to bind the moss in place.

The Wildlife and Countryside Act 1981 protects nearly all wild birds' eggs from being taken from their nests. There are a few exceptions, including the lapwing (or green plover), whose eggs may be collected until 14 April and used for home consumption although they may not be sold. The eggs of the collared dove, which was introduced to Britain in the mid-1950s from the Middle East, and some gulls' eggs may also be eaten. Gulls' eggs are considered a great delicacy, but they may be collected by authorized people only, and gulls' eggs can be sold under licence for human consumption between mid-March and mid-May. Some specialist delicatessens sell them ready-cooked, but if you want to prepare them yourself, cook them in boiling water for 10 minutes, when the whites will look slightly blue and the yolks will be very deep, almost orange, yellow. They have a fine taste and are traditionally served quite simply with celery salt and brown bread and butter.

All game birds have tough shells and, rather surprisingly, have a slightly fishy taste. They are well worth trying and can usually be bought from licensed game dealers. Pheasants' eggs can be hard boiled and used in salads (cook them for 3 minutes in boiling water). Partridge eggs, which taste just as good, can be prepared in the same way.

THE BREAKFAST TRAY

Yet surely in the morning of the world there must have been bacon and eggs and marmalade. Else why did the first sleeper waken?
T. Earle Welby

This type of breakfast offers an opportunity to devote an hour or two to the good things of life – the Sunday papers while you listen to the gentle sizzling of bacon and sausages as they cook gently on a hob; the wonderful aroma of fresh-ground coffee; the rich, buttery fragrance of croissants warming in the oven; and the casual elegance of a table set with fine china, fresh linen and a small posy of fresh flowers.

MENU
Freshly squeezed orange juice
Fried eggs, bacon, sausage, tomatoes
Pan-fried new potatoes
Warm croissants served with
Nectarine and Passion Fruit Curd
Coffee with hot milk

EGGS
Find a supplier of really fresh, free-range eggs with a good flavour. When you break them into the pan the yolks will look full and rounded, the whites firm and thick. Old eggs will spread out, thin and flat, when you break them into the pan.

Add 1 heaped tbsp of clean fat for each egg and 1 tsp of butter for extra flavour. Set the fat over a moderate heat and when it is hot, reduce to a low heat as eggs respond well to slow cooking. Crack the egg close to the fat into the pan. Splash fat over the egg, especially over the white, until it begins to set. When the egg is cooked, gently slide it on a spatula out of the pan. Drain off the fat by briefly resting both spatula and egg on kitchen paper, then serve.

BACON
Choose freshly sliced bacon, cut from the bone by a good family butcher, preferably one who cures his own. Traditionally, bacon is cured in a solution of salt and brine, but some specialist bacons have molasses and beer in the brine, which gives a deliciously sweet flavour. Bacon can be smoked or unsmoked (or green). Smoking enhances the flavour.

Do not buy bacon that produces a milky substance when you cook it. This is caused by too much water, which is added by the processors to increase the weight of the bacon, and as it cooks the bacon shrivels up like a dry, stiff leaf.

For a clean flavour and less fat, cook bacon under the full heat of the grill until the fatty edge turns golden and the centre looks cooked but is still succulent.

CROSS TOMATOES
Small tomatoes look pretty prepared in this way. Use a sharp knife to take a small slice from the stalk end and then cut a small cross on the top of the rounded end. Set the tomatoes under a hot grill, cross side up. Cook them with the bacon because they take about the same time, and leave them in the oven on a covered plate until you need them.

SAUSAGES
Sausages are made from a mixture of lean and fat meat, flavoured with pungent spices and sometimes herbs. Sausages must contain at least 65 per cent meat, but good ones usually have a higher proportion of lean meat, although some fat is necessary to keep them succulent. Unless you make your own, you will probably find the best sausages from a family butcher, when they will have a natural casing, which I find cooks better than those made with an artificial casing, which browns too quickly.

Add the fat to a frying pan and set over a moderate heat. Drop in the sausage and allow them to sizzle energetically for a few seconds as they puff up into their full shape. Then turn down the heat to very low, and allow the sausages to cook slowly. You will need to turn them frequently.

POTATOES
It is always something of a treat to have potatoes at breakfast time, and warmed left-over Potato Dauphinoise (see page 46)

or cooked cold salad potatoes, sautéed in butter, go exceedingly well with a cooked breakfast.

RISE AND SHINE IN A BLUEBELL WOOD

Mouthwatering fresh fruit shakes and scrambled eggs with smoked salmon are rounded off with American breakfast muffins and praline-flavoured coffee.

FRUIT SHAKES
INGREDIENTS
1 mango
600ml/1pt freshly squeezed orange juice
(about 8 oranges)
freshly squeezed lime juice to taste

Peel, stone and roughly cut the mango into small cubes. Place in the goblet of a blender and add the orange juice. Blend until smooth, then sharpen the flavour with lime juice. Chill, then pour into serving glasses.

SCRAMBLED EGGS WITH SMOKED SALMON
INGREDIENTS
4 slices smoked salmon
8 farm-fresh eggs
2 tbsp milk
25g/1oz butter
salt and freshly ground pepper
several chives

Divide the salmon into four equal portions and arrange one portion on the side of each plate.

Break the eggs into a bowl and beat with a fork. Strain the eggs and milk into a separate bowl. Melt the butter in a saucepan over low to moderate heat until it begins to foam lightly. Add the egg and milk mix and reduce the heat slightly. Cook gently, stirring constantly with a large spoon to fold the edges of the mixture towards the centre until it forms golden, creamy flakes. Season. Scoop out the eggs onto the four plates next to the salmon and garnish with freshly snipped chives. Serve immediately.

MORNING GLORY MUFFINS

The ingredients – as is appropriate for an American recipe – are given in cups, which is a convenient way of indicating proportions. Use a cup that holds 140g/5oz (which is the equivalent of about 200ml/ 8fl oz of liquid).

EQUIPMENT
muffin tins

INGREDIENTS
1¾ cups plain flour
2 tsp baking powder
½ tsp salt
3 well-rounded tbsp golden caster sugar
¼ cup melted butter
2 eggs
grated rind of 1 orange
½ cup freshly squeezed orange and grapefruit juice (equal amounts of each)

MARMALADE GLAZE
25g/1oz butter
25g/1oz caster sugar
1–2 tbs thin-cut marmalade

Mix the dry ingredients in a bowl. Slowly melt the butter, then leave it for about 5 minutes to cool slightly. Lightly beat the eggs, then stir in the melted butter, orange rind and fresh juice. Pour over the centre of the dry ingredients and fold in gently with a large wooden spoon until just blended. Do not overwork the mixture.

Spoon the mix into muffin tins. Grease the tins all over the surface as well as in the indentations. You can also use large muffin paper cases, but I use two cases for each muffin because the mixture is quite heavy. Do not fill the cases right up to the top.

Bake in a preheated oven at 200°C/ 400°F/gas mark 6 for 20 minutes. Remove from the oven and, if they are in tins, carefully turn them out. Leave to cool slightly. Meanwhile, slowly heat the butter, sugar and marmalade together until the sugar has melted. Dribble a little glaze over the top of each muffin, using the back of a teaspoon to make sure that it covers the surface evenly.

PRALINE COFFEE
Make a medium brew of your normal coffee, but add 1 tbsp of praline powder (see page 81) to every 1 tbsp of ground coffee to the filter bag or percolator.

NECTARINE AND PASSION FRUIT CURD

INGREDIENTS
6 passion fruits
1 ripe, medium sized nectarine, peeled
55g/2oz butter
110g/4oz caster sugar
1½ tbsp freshly squeezed lime juice
grated zest of ½ lime
4 egg yolks and 1 egg white, from
farm-fresh eggs slightly whisked

A bowl of good marmalade is hard to beat at breakfast, but for special occasions add a zing to the warmed, fresh croissants or hot buttered toast with this curd. Choose passion fruit with deeply wrinkled skins, which will show that they are ripe.

Cut open the passion fruit and scoop out the fleshy seeds into a small sieve set over a bowl. Use the back of a spoon to scrape and press the juice from the seeds. Although you will only get a little juice, it is powerful and aromatic. Whiz the juice and nectarine flesh together in a liquidizer and add the contents to a small saucepan. Add the other ingredients and stir the mixture over a moderate heat until it thickens and becomes like thick cream. Remove from the heat immediately and pour into a clean jam jar. Seal and chill in the fridge to set and thicken. It will keep for several weeks.

If you leave it for too long after it comes to the boil the mixture will curdle. Cook over a double boiler if you like to have more control over this stage.

BOULE DE MEULE

INGREDIENTS
1kg/2¼lb unbleached stoneground flour
20g/¾oz fresh yeast or 12g/½oz
dried yeast
650ml/23fl oz water at 25°C/77°F
(checked with a thermometer)
2 tsp salt

PÂTE À DÉCOR
600g/1¼lb white flower
65g/2½ oz butter or margarine, softened
250–300ml/9–10fl oz cold water

French bread artist Jacky Lesellier gave me this recipe. His family have been making bread and pastries in the French town of Honfleur since 1721, and he now has a successful shop, the Bagatelle Boutique, in London, which supplies many distinguished hotels, restaurants and delicatessens.

The care taken in preparation and the use of top quality ingredients make this bread superior in both taste and texture. The appealing grape-vine motif, made with a pâte à décor (decor dough), is an echo of the autumn harvest festivals in France, although you can use any other seasonal pattern just as successfully.

Pour the flour onto your work surface and shape it into a well. Put the yeast into the centre of the well and dissolve it with some of the water. The best method is to smooth the yeast into the water with your fingertips, working in a slow circular movement to make a wet paste in the well of the flour. Gradually draw in more of the flour with the water and salt to make a soft dough. Knead by hand, repeatedly dropping the dough hard onto a floured working surface, stretching and folding it, then dropping it and kneading it again on the work surface.

Work like this for 15 minutes to incorporate the air, then shape it into a smooth ball and cover it with a damp cloth or a piece of plastic film. Leave for 1 hour in a warm place.

Make the *pâte à décor*. Place the flour on your working surface and make a well in the centre as before. Add some water and the butter and smooth it into the water to make a soft paste. Draw in the flour with more water until it is combined in the dough. Knead lightly for 5 minutes to make a smooth dough but not to incorporate air. Leave covered in plastic for about 45 minutes.

Meanwhile, return to the bread dough. Stretch and knock back the dough for about 30 seconds to eliminate the air and re-form it into a smooth ball. Cover with a damp cloth or a piece of plastic film again and leave for 34–40 minutes. Knock back and reshape the dough again for 30 seconds, making a smooth ball. Cover this with a damp cloth or plastic as before and leave for 45 minutes.

Take a small piece of the *pâte à décor* and roll it into a thin, flat piece, roughly the shape of a bunch of grapes. Mould small balls of dough to be the grapes. Use a pastry brush to dampen

the surface of the flat shape with water and press over it the small balls to form a bunch of grapes. Make a second shape in the same way. Cut away the excess dough around the edges with a sharp knife. Roll two pieces of dough into small sausages, moulding them to look like vine stalks, with a smaller piece protruding from the centre of each. Dampen and attach the stalks to the underside of the bunches of grapes. Thinly roll out four small pieces of dough and cut out four vine leaves, using a real vine leaf as a template if you can (some good delicatessens sell paper ones, but a large ivy leaf will do instead). Dampen the leaves and attach them.

Cut small strips to form thin sausage shapes, 1 x 7.5cm/½ x 3in, and pull out one end so that it resembles a stalk. Use scissors to make a series of snips along the widest edge, one in the centre and one at each side. Set the decorations on a sheet lined with silicone paper and freeze to harden.

Prepare and shape the bread for the oven. Knock back and shape the dough for 30 seconds and leave it covered for 5–10 minutes, then form it on a metal baking sheet lined with silicone paper. The dough should be about 2.5cm/1in thick and 12in/30cm across. Leave in a warm place for a further 1½ –2 hours, covered with a damp cloth or a piece of plastic film.

Preheat the oven to 220°C/425°F/ gas mark 7, and place a meat roasting tin filled with boiling water on the lower shelf to create steam. Use a pair of scissors to snip all round the edge and make sharp stabs all over the surface of the dough. Paint the dough with water and bake for 25 minutes. Remove the bread from the oven and paint water over the surface once more. Take the decorations straight from the freezer and press them quickly in place on the surface of the bread. Return the bread to the oven and bake for a further 20 minutes. Reduce the temperature to 180°C/350°F/gas mark 4 and bake for a further 20–30 minutes until the bread is mid-brown and sounds hollow when the base is tapped. Cover the bread loosely with kitchen foil towards the end of cooking if it browns too quickly.

DINNER ROLLS SERVED IN A BREAD BASKET

Freshly baked bread rolls, lightly dusted with flour and served in a plaited bread basket, make a stylish and memorable addition to the dinner table. To make the basket you will need a mandrin – a board with metal rods – which you can buy from specialist chef suppliers.

For the rolls, use the ingredients for the basic Boule de Meule (see page 62) and work them into a smooth dough by dropping, stretching and folding as described for 15 minutes. Shape the dough into small ovals, cover with a damp cloth and leave for 1 hour in a warm place. Use scissors to make

4–6 snips along the top of the dough ovals, dust with flour and bake, above a steam bath, for 18–20 minutes in a preheated oven at 220°C/425°F/ gas mark 7.

Make the *pâte à décor* as described in the previous recipe.

Generously butter the base and around the rods of the basket mould. Cut the *pâte à décor* dough into strips, and roll out several of them into long, sausage shapes about 1cm/½in thick and 90–120cm/3–4ft or more long if your working surface permits. Take the first strip and press the end of it firmly to the centre of the buttered base. Then begin to wind it into a tight oval coil, pressing it to the base until you reach the metal rods. Continue to work with the long strips, weaving them in and out of the rods until you reach the height you want. To finish off, tuck the end under the strip below on the inside.

You can paint the basket with egg glaze for a shiny finish or leave it *au naturel* – either way is equally effective. Bake at 220°C/425°F/gas mark 7 for 30 minutes until it is golden brown. Remove from the oven and leave to cool for a few minutes before carefully pulling out the rods from the top. The basket will last indefinitely if it is handled gently, but it will become increasingly fragile with age.

BUTTER

Dairy maids used to demonstrate the skills learned in cool dairies by making shapes to decorate farm shop windows or food stalls at country fairs. Their skilled hands created beautiful swans, towers and baskets containing intricately carved flowers. Smaller, round pats were often decorated with impressed motifs to advertise the farm at which the butter had been made. These motifs generally took the form of corn stooks, strawberries and even milkmaids, and they were moulded on wooden butter stamps. These more ornate stamps gradually gave way to wooden butter 'hands', which impressed a simple striped pattern as the butter was slapped and formed into squares.

Nowadays decorated butters have fallen from favour, and plain squares wrapped in foil and parchment have taken their place. However, we can produce decorative butter quite easily, using modern butter hands and the handful of rubber, plastic and tin moulds that are available in good kitchen ware shops.

Home-made butter will produce a delicious yellow butter, with a richness that is reminiscent of the more flavoursome butter that will be familiar to those of us who stayed on a dairy farm in our childhood or who live near a dairy farm shop that specializes in home-made products.

PREPARING MOULDED BUTTER

Take the butter from the fridge and leave it to stand at room temperature for 1 hour. Further soften it by mashing it with a fork until it is creamy. The butter shapes can be made well in advance and stored between silicone paper in a rigid plastic box in a freezer for 3 months or more. You can defrost them as required to accompany a variety of different dishes – as garnishes for hot food or set in pretty porcelain butter dishes to serve with bread.

SMALL DECORATIVE MOULDS

Rinse rubber butter moulds or rigid plastic moulds of the kind that are generally used for making sweets in cold water, then press softened butter into the moulds, firmly and evenly. Chill rubber moulds and freeze rigid ones. When you need to de-mould, press your fingers into the backs of the pliable moulds or hold a rigid mould for 2–3 seconds in luke warm water and follow as for tin moulds.

SMALL TIN MOULDS

Use as the rubber moulds, but when you need to release the shapes you will have to insert the tip of a knife between the still frozen butter and the mould to ease it carefully out.

WOODEN STAMPS

These are still made for moulding butter and can be found in good kitchen ware shops. You may also be fortunate enough to find some original stamps in antique shops. They are generally made in sycamore, which does not flavour food or distort as it becomes damp, because the stamp must be rinsed in cold water before it is pressed into the butter. Leave for several hours before removing the stamp.

PLAIN DISCS

Form the softened butter into a roll with wetted butter hands, wrap it in silicone paper and freeze. Cut off slices as required.

MAKING FLAVOURED BUTTERS

Butter combines so well with other flavours that it is something of a challenge to invent new associations that can be frozen and kept ready to

garnish appropriate dishes. Whenever possible, mould the shapes according to the dish – for example, butter moulded into small shells could accompany fish or scented butter could be moulded into flower shapes to serve with fresh scones.

MAKING YOUR OWN BUTTER
Butter used to be made in glass jar churns with wooden paddles, and you can still find these in sales of kitchen bric-à-brac, but it is so easy to make in an electric mixer and the taste, colour and texture are so superior to the butter found in supermarkets that it is worth making your own for really special occasions. Use about 1.1l/2pt of rich whipping cream and overwhip it until it separates into small globules of fat. Reduce the speed and continue to mix until the globules stick together, leaving the pale, thin buttermilk in the bottom of the bowl. Drain this away and use it when you are making scones or soda bread.

Remove any remaining buttermilk by washing the butter in clean running water, either by squishing it with wetted butter hands on a sloping board standing near the sink or by turning it into a piece of muslin and holding it under the tap while you squeeze it gently until the water runs clear. Unless you have a strong preference for unsalted butter, now add ½ tsp of salt to every 450g/1lb of butter, using the butter hands to blend it thoroughly.

FRUIT AND SCENTED BUTTERS
Blend together 110g/4oz of softened butter with as much sweetened strawberry purée, or any other fruit purée or your choice, as it will take and still hold its shape. Press it into small

rubber moulds and freeze. De-mould and defrost before serving with fresh, warmed scones.

Also try chopping and pounding pretty orange marigold or sweet geranium petals into the same amount of butter. Add 1 tsp of honey and several drops of flower water to make the perfect accompaniment for wild fruit jelly and warm scones.

CINNAMON TOAST BUTTER
Blend 225g/8oz of softened butter with 4 tsp of ground cinnamon, a large pinch of ground cloves, a large pinch of ground ginger and 4 tbsp of light muscovado sugar. Spread the soft mixture into a thin, even layer over silicone paper and leave to harden in the fridge or freezer. Use a decorative biscuit cutter – a heart-shape would be pretty – to stamp out the butter, which should be served with piping hot toast.

HONEY HAZELNUT AND
BRANDY BUTTER
Grill 80g/3oz of hazelnuts until the skins are lightly charred, then rub them briskly in a tea towel to remove the skins. Crush them finely before mixing with 80g/3oz of softened butter, 55g/2oz of caster sugar and 1 tbsp of brandy. Freeze in discs and defrost for an instant individual filling for a freshly cooked crêpe or to melt over a small steamed sponge pudding.

SWEET LEMON BUTTER STICKS
Blend together 110g/4oz of softened butter with the juice and zest of 1 small lemon and 2–3 tsp of caster sugar, with salt and pepper to season. Cut evenly sized rectangles from a slab of butter and form them into long, criss-cross patterned cylinders by rolling them between wetted ribbed butter hands. Use these as a last-minute addition, melting over a bowl of freshly cooked garden peas or young carrots.

ICE AND FRUIT

As we saw in the section on vegetables, food that is garden-fresh does not need elaborate presentation. Strawberries or raspberries set on a fine china plate with a relief pattern of strawberry blossom and a tiny dipping well to fill with sugar or cream are unbeatable.

RED SUMMER FRUITS
Make up a light syrup by boiling together water, sugar and a splash of liqueur, such as grenadine or cassis, and add the thin, red, warm syrup over strawberries, redcurrants or raspberries or a mixture or all three before serving with clotted cream.

If you like more elaborate accessories, try the beautifully cheesy, slightly acidic flavour of a creamy white, heart-shaped *coeur la crème* or Fruits au Gratin (see page 92), using sliced strawberries instead of the mixed fruit. A more cooling accompaniment would be raspberry sorbet.

A RAINBOW OF SORBETS
After several years' apprenticeship at the Patisserie Peltier, one of the top five patisseries in Paris, Julian Tomkins founded La Maison des Sorbets in London in 1982 to make the finest quality sorbets, which are notable both their exquisite taste and their beautiful presentation. It seemed appropriate that I should ask Julian for advice about the best way to freeze sorbets in natural, frosted fruit skins (see page 74).

The sorbets are made with fruit and a thin syrup of sugar and water, which is churned in a sorbetière to keep the mixture moving evenly and slowly as it freezes. In the absence of a sorbetière, it is quite easy to follow the basic recipe, beating the mixture twice during the freezing process to break down the ice crystals. Adjust the quantities of sugar and lemon according to the acidity of the fruit you use.

BASIC SORBET

EQUIPMENT
a shallow metal container, preferably a bowl, that fits into your freezer

INGREDIENTS
200g/7oz sugar
300ml/½pt water
300ml/½pt pure fruit juice (or the equivalent in puréed fruit pulp made from about 450g/1lb fruit)
juice of one lemon

Turn your freezer or the freezing compartment of your refrigerator to its coldest about 1 hour before the mixture will be ready for freezing. Place the metal container in the freezer.

Put the sugar and water in a saucepan and heat gently until the sugar has dissolved. Boil, without stirring, for 3 minutes. Remove from the heat and leave to cool.

Add the fruit juice (or the puréed equivalent) and lemon juice to the cooled syrup. Take the container from the freezer, fill it with the mixture and return it to the freezer. Leave it until the mixture is hard around the edges but slushy in the centre, take it from the freezer and beat it vigorously to break down the ice crystals. This is best done with an electric beater, but you can use a balloon whisk. Return the mixture to the freezer until it has the same half-frozen appearance as before. Beat it again, then cover the container with a double lid of kitchen foil and refreeze.

VARIATIONS ON THE BASIC SORBET

Apple
Use Cox's Pippins for the best flavour and add 2 tbsp of calvados to the basic recipe (see Apple Swan Sorbet, page 76).

Kiwi Fruit
You will need the juice of only ½ a lemon.

Lemon
Make with 300ml/½pt lemon juice and add an extra 25g/1oz of sugar.

Lychees
Lychees or longans (dragon's eyes) are available in tins in Chinese food stores. Reduce the amount of sugar to 110g/4oz. You will need one large tin of fruit, drained and puréed, mixed with 3 tbsp of ginger wine.

Orange or Maltese Orange
The Maltese or blood orange has a glorious deep red pulp. The sweetly acidic juice of oranges makes exceedingly flavoursome sorbets. Follow the basic recipe.

Peach
For an extra-luxurious sorbet replace about two-thirds of the water with champagne.

Raspberry and Strawberry
Follow the basic recipe for both these fruits for deliciously summery sorbets.

Pear
Purée 350g/12oz of pears, preferably William pears, and add the juice of only ½ a lemon and 2 tbsp of pear liqueur. As an optional luxury, add 8–10 chopped *marron glacés*.

Pineapple
Use the juice of only ½ a lemon and add 2 tbsp of kirsch.

Pink Grapefruit
If you cannot obtain pink grapefruit, add 1–2 tbsp of grenadine to the grapefruit juice. Remember to leave out the lemon juice, because white grapefruit is tarter than its pink relation. Follow the basic recipe.

Tamarillo
Follow the basic recipe.

VANILLA, GINGER, HONEY AND SAFFRON ICE-CREAM BOMBE

EQUIPMENT
bombe mould, cake tin or a rectangular tin with a capacity of about 1.1l/2pt

INGREDIENTS
VANILLA ICE-CREAM
600ml/1pt milk
1 vanilla pod, split lengthways
6 egg yolks
170g/6oz caster sugar
300ml/½pt double cream

GINGER, HONEY AND SAFFRON ICE-CREAM
600ml/1pt milk
1 small jar crystallized ginger
1 tbsp ginger syrup from the crystallized ginger
5 tbsp strong-flavoured honey
1¼ tsp ground ginger
generous pinch of saffron strands
6 egg yolks
200ml/7fl oz double cream

Make the vanilla ice-cream by heating together the milk and vanilla pod. Just before it reaches boiling point, remove it from the heat allow the pod to infuse for 20 minutes. Remove the pod. Use an electric beater or a balloon whisk to beat the egg yolks and sugar together until the sugar has dissolved and the mixture is smooth and creamy. Slowly pour the warm milk into the egg mixture, whisking all the time. Return the mixture to the saucepan and cook over a low heat, stirring continuously, until it has the consistency of a thin custard and will coat the back of the a spoon. Leave the custard to one side, stirring occasionally, until it cools. Beat the cream until it just forms soft peaks and fold it into the cooled custard. Freeze as for sorbets (see page 70).

Make the ginger, saffron and honey ice-cream by bringing the milk to the boil and removing it immediately from the heat. Stir in 55g/2oz of finely chopped ginger, the ginger syrup, the honey and ground ginger. Sprinkle the saffron on top and leave to one side for the saffron to infuse. Whisk the eggs in a bowl and stir in the saffron- and ginger-flavoured milk. Return to the saucepan and cook over a lower heat to make the custard base. Then follow the same method as for the vanilla ice-cream.

Chill the tin and add a layer about 12mm/½ in deep of vanilla ice-cream, softened at room temperature and further softened with a large spoon, in the base. Freeze to harden. Use a metal spatula to line the sides with a 12mm/½in layer of softened vanilla ice-cream. Use the back of a spoon to form the rounded contours at the base of the bombe mould if you are using one. Return the tin to the freezer, checking from time to time in case the ice-cream slips down the side. Press it back in place with a spoon before it freezes.

When the outer layer has frozen, add a 12mm/½in layer of softened ginger ice-cream to the central cavity. Freeze until solid, then dot some slices of crystallized ginger cut into halves and quarters over the surface then add a 2.5cm/1in thick layer of softened ginger ice-cream, smoothing it down between the ginger pieces and into the contours of the tin with a spatula. Freeze. Dot with another layer of ginger and continue to fill the mould in the same way until the ice-cream is about 12mm/½in from the top of the mould. Freeze, then finish off with a layer of vanilla ice-cream, levelling off the top with a palette knife. Cover with a double layer of kitchen foil. Freeze until firm. To demould dip the mould into warm water and turn out on a serving dish.

FILLED FRUIT SHELLS WITH SORBET

Before you begin this recipe – à la Maison des Sorbets – it is worth freezing a fruit you want to use to see how well it freezes. You will find that those with harder skins, such as the lemon, pink grapefruit, orange and apple shown here, are best for this particular kind of presentation.

INGREDIENTS
fruit of your choice

SYRUP
225g/8oz granulated sugar
200ml/6fl oz water

Prepare the syrup by adding the sugar and water to a saucepan. Bring to the boil, whisking the sugar into the water to prevent it sticking or burning, then allow to boil for several minutes. Leave to cool.

Cut away a small slice from the underside of the fruit of your choice so that it sits level on your working surface. You will need to do this before freezing the fruit – it will be impossible once it is frozen solid. Halve the fruit and scrape out the flesh and pith, reserving the juices for use in the sorbet. Brush the inside of the fruit thoroughly with the syrup, allowing any excess to drain off. Then freeze the shells.

Adding a coating of syrup to the insides of the shells prevents the sorbet from being tainted by any bitterness leaching through from the skin and it prevents oxidization and discoloration.

Fill the shells with the sorbet, slightly softened and moulded to form a similar shape to the top of the shell. Open freeze for just long enough for the sorbet to become firm, then cover with freezer bags and refreeze until you are ready to use them.

LACY TUILES
These are the ideal accompaniment for apple sorbet (see page 76).

MAKES 4 TUILES

INGREDIENTS
55g/2oz demerara sugar
55g/2oz unsalted butter
40g/1½oz almonds, finely chopped

Preheat the oven to 190°C/375°F/gas mark 5. Slowly melt the sugar and butter together in a small saucepan, stirring continuously, for 2–3 minutes. Add the almonds and stir for a further ½ minute. Divide the mixture into four more or less equal portions and spread two portions well apart on a lightly greased baking sheet and bake for 5 minutes. Remove from the oven and leave to cool for 1½–2 minutes until you can lift them with palette knife.

Press the warm biscuits over a rolling pin or drape them over up-turned cups, coaxing the edges to form a frill. Cook the other two biscuits in the same say. You can store the tuiles for several days in an airtight tin.

APPLE SWAN SORBET WITH CALVADOS SABAYON

Apple swans are a delightful garnish for this apple sorbet, which is accompanied by a thick, foaming sabayon and flavoured with a dash of calvados, which rounds out the flavour perfectly. Make the sabayon just before serving. Fortunately, the sorbet can be prepared in advance, and the apple swans will keep for several hours if you stored them in acidulated water to stop the flesh becoming discoloured. You will need a very sharp knife to cut out the little fanned sections of apple that form the swan's wings and tail.

SERVES 4

INGREDIENTS
1 quantity apple sorbet (see page 71)
4 ripe, red unblemished, medium sized apples

CALVADOS SABAYON
3 egg yolks
1 tbsp dry white wine
1 tbsp caster sugar
1 dssp calvados

Make the apple swans by washing and drying the apples on a clean tea towel. Lay the apple on its side and cut a slice away from the bottom, just under the stalk. Reserve this slice in acidulated water.

Place the apple on its flat side and cut the first wing by holding your knife at an angle of 45 degrees and making a small eye-shaped cut, slanting upwards, into the side of the apple. Keep the knife at the same angle and make another, slightly larger cut around it. Make the same cut shapes on the other side of the apple to make the other wing.

Form the tail by making a similar small, eye-shaped cut into the centre at the top of the apple. This time, make two more similarly shaped cuts around it, leaving a small margin between each one. Carve out the swan's head and neck from the reserved piece of apple, and cut a small V-shaped slot in the front of the apple to accommodate it. Finally, carefully press and fan out the cut shapes to create the wings and tails.

Transfer the sorbet from the freezer to the fridge to allow it to soften for about 20 minutes before you need to assemble the pudding.

Make the sabayon by putting all the ingredients into a bowl and whisking them together thoroughly. Set the bowl over a pan of simmering water above a double boiler and whisk smartly for about 3 minutes until the mixture thickens into a mousse-like sauce or leaves a ribbon trail when the whisk is lifted. Take care: the sauce will curdle if it gets too hot.

Serve the sauce while it is still warm or, if you prefer, whisk it over iced water until it is cold. It will hold its shape quite well for about 45 minutes.

Pour the sabayon over four dessert plates. Add a spoonful of sorbet, moulded between two spoons, to the tuile (see page 74) and add a swan to each plate to glide gracefully on the sauce. Add a dusting of icing sugar and serve.

MINIATURE TARTS OF ART

MAKES 16

EQUIPMENT
small tartlet tins, lightly greased with butter

INGREDIENTS
110g/4oz plain flour
40g/1½oz caster sugar
pinch of salt
55g/2oz butter
2 egg yolks
1 tsp vanilla essence

CRÈME PATISSIÈRE
2 tbsp cornflour
3 tbsp plain flour
55g/2oz caster sugar
300ml/½pt milk
2 large eggs, beaten
½ tsp vanilla essence
1 tbsp kirsch
½ tsp unsalted butter
150ml/5fl oz double cream

FRUIT DECORATION
a selection of fruits, including mango, kiwi fruit (Chinese gooseberries), strawberries, cherries and red-, white- or blackcurrants and blackberries.

Perfect French pastry tartlet shells are filled with crème patissière *and pretty arrangements of fruit, then painted with a glaze to make tiny, sparkling jewel cases that look almost too good to eat. Larger tartlets can be made by doubling the quantities and tin sizes.*

Sift the flour on a board or marble slab and make an open well in the centre. Place the sugar, salt, butter, egg yolks and vanilla in the well. Use the fingertips of one hand in a pecking motion to work the eggs and butter mixture together until it resembles scrambled eggs. Gradually draw in the flour, and continue to combine the ingredients until the mixture is crumb-like.

Gather the mixture into a moist ball and lightly knead it on a floured surface for 30 seconds, pushing the dough away from you with the heel of your hand and drawing it back until the pastry is smooth. Do not overwork the dough or it will become greasy. Wrap it in soft kitchen paper and a plastic bag and leave it in the fridge for 45 minutes.

Prepare the *crème patissière*. Mix the cornflour, flour and sugar to a smooth paste with a little of the milk in a pan.

Add the beaten egg yolks and gradually whisk in the remaining milk until the ingredients are well combined. Continue to whisk over a medium heat. The mixture will thicken unevenly before slightly thinning out to a smooth paste. Beat in the vanilla and kirsch, then remove it from the heat. Transfer the mixture to a glass or china bowl and rub the warm surface with a small knob of butter, which will help prevent a skin from forming. Leave to cool.

Whisk the cream until it barely holds its shape, then use an electric whisk to beat in the cold custard until it is perfectly smooth. Cover and set aside.

Roll out the pastry thinly and line the pastry cases. Line with soft kitchen tissue and baking beans and cook in a preheated oven at 200°C/400°F/gas mark 6 for 8–9 minutes. Remove the tissue and beans and bake for a further 5 minutes. Leave to cool slightly before turning out onto a wire cake rack.

Use a six-star nozzle fitted to a pastry bag to pipe *crème patissière* into the pastry case and carefully arrange the fruit on top. Glaze with hot apricot or crabapple glaze.

SUGARCRAFT

Sugar is generally used for making desserts, and it comes in various shades, textures and flavours. It is worth keeping several different kinds in your store cupboard to make instant decorations and toppings for all kinds of sweet dishes. You can make an unusual gift by layering different sugars (see Carnival Sugar, opposite). The idea comes from a shop in Paris that specializes in sugar products, and it is rather reminiscent of the lovely shaped glass jars filled with layers of different coloured sand that you used to be able to buy in some seaside towns. When you are making flavoured sugars, leave them to permeate for about 2 weeks before using them.

VANILLA SUGAR

The vanilla pod is the seed pod of a climbing orchid (*Vanilla planifolia*), which is native to Mexico. Put several bruised vanilla pods, or one fresh and some used (washed and dried), in a screw-top jar filled with caster sugar and leave until the vanilla's heady, exotic fragrance has permeated the sugar. Home-made vanilla sugar adds a most exquisite flavour to *crème brûlée* (see Goose Egg Crème Brûlée, page 88), crème caramel, *crème à l'anglaise*,

chantilly cream, semolina and many other sweet dishes. It is even quite pleasant in weak tea, particularly with a black tea, such as Ceylon or Assam, or a China tea.

CANDY SUGAR

Tea connoisseurs who like to sweeten their tea just a little without masking the tea's subtle flavours find candy sugar is ideal. It sweetens without flavouring, but it takes longer to dissolve. (Tea drinkers should also look at the recipe for Citrus Sugar, page 81.)

MUSCOVADO

Choose the best unrefined cane sugar as marked on the packet. The two main types are light and dark. Dark muscovado has a strong taste, like burnt toffee. Some health food restaurants used to leave it in bowls on tables for their customers to use to sweeten their tea: the result is horrendous. However, it does taste good in rich fruit and ginger cakes, and it is also a main ingredient in a basting cure for sweet cured ham.

Light muscovado is a soft, mid-brown colour with a mild molasses flavour, and it is ideal for melting deliciously over hot porridge, semolina and rice puddings. It is also one of the chief ingredients of toffee and fudge. Do try it in meringues.

Fold in equal quantities of light muscovado and caster sugar as an alternative to all-white sugar into stiffly beaten egg whites for a richer tasting and more unusual coffee-coloured meringue. This will be a beautiful complement to the pale ivory cream filling that is used to hold them together. Try adding 1 dssp of either praline or vanilla sugar to 300ml/½pt of cream for the filling.

PRALINE

This is reminiscent of almond brittle that has been crushed into a fine powder. It can be used as a flavouring for ice-creams, cream and cold soufflés and for the cream filling for those elaborate little cakes and gateaux that decorate the finest patisserie windows, when it is known as *crème pralinée*.

Place equal amounts of granulated sugar and almonds (blanched or unblanched) in a heavy pan and cook over a very low heat until the sugar has caramelized into a deep golden syrup. Pour onto a lightly oiled baking sheet, spread it out thinly and leave to cool. When it is hard, break it into pieces and put the pieces in a plastic bag. Pulverize them with a rolling pin or something similar until it is a fine powder. It is now ready to use or it can be kept in a screw-top jar.

CARNIVAL SUGAR

In the nineteenth century carnival glass was made with the bits of coloured glass left at the end of the day in the glass factories. The brightly coloured strands and bits of glass were melted down to form vases and other small decorative objects, which were then sold at fairs and carnivals. This sugar reminds me of that glass.

To make a coloured sugar, add several drops of natural food colouring to a glass jam jar containing 55g/2oz of granulated sugar and shake vigorously for 3–4 minutes until the sugar is evenly coloured.

Make three of more colours in this way. Stand a small glass jar so that it is tilted at an angle, resting it on, say, a small biscuit cutter, then carefully add half the quantity of coloured sugars in layered swirls until the jar is full. Smooth the top layer smooth with a knife, screw on the top of the jar and store in a dry place. Add a spoonful as a final touch to sponges or trifles or to cheer up the rather bland face of a bowl of rice pudding.

CITRUS SUGAR

Rub sugar cubes roughly over the skins of several oranges and a lemon to remove the colour and zest – *zeste* is the French word for 'peel', the exterior, coloured and flavoured part of the skin of an orange, lemon, tangerine and so on. Set the cubes on a tray and dry them in a warm oven. Place the cubes between folded paper and crush them to a fine powder with a rolling pin. This sugar can be added to the ingredients of light cakes and sponges.

Alternatively, break the cubes lightly into small rough pieces, rather similar to coffee crystals, and use it as a crunchy topping to rock cakes and bread pudding. Or you could place them in a screw-top jar with strips of thinly cut orange and lemon rinds with the pith removed. Refresh the peel as necessary.

Try Citrus Sugar as a delicate flavouring for tea such as Darjeeling, Ceylon or Assam, or for a green tea.

LAVENDER SUGAR

This can be used to add a gentle fragrance to a sorbet, ice-cream or cream. Pick a small handful of lavender heads and leave them in a warm airing-cupboard or on a sunny windowsill for 4–5 hours. Add them to 225g/8oz caster sugar and bruise roughly with a knife. Spread the resulting mixture over a large plate and leave it to dry, again on a warm windowsill or in an airing-cupboard. Place in a screw-top jam jar.

ROSE PETAL SUGAR

Choose fragrant red garden roses, preferably the large-flowered ones, because cluster roses have less scent. Pick off their petals and spread them on a large plate in the warmth of a sunny windowsill or in an airing-cupboard to remove some of the moisture. Follow the instructions for Lavender Sugar (above) except that you should add several drops of rose-scented water to the sugar and shake them together in a jar for several minutes until it permeates right through the sugar. Several dried flowerheads, pressed between the jar and the sugar, will look very pretty if you make them as a gift, and you could give it a pale pink tint (see Carnival Sugar, above).

SPICED SUGAR

Place cinnamon bark, broken roughly into small pieces, ginger, nutmeg, cardamon seeds from the pods and cloves in a coffee grinder and grind them into a fine powder. Add 1 rounded tbsp to 225g/8oz caster sugar in a screw-top jar and leave it to allow the spicy aroma to permeate the sugar. This is ideal for Easter recipes such as simnel cake or hot cross buns.

SPUN SUGAR, CARAMEL CAGES AND GLAZED FRUIT

To caramelize means to melt sugar into a syrup (see Goose Egg Crème Brûlée, page 88). If the syrup is cooked to a higher temperature it can be formed into crisp, free-form caramel decorations or a web-like floss, which can be lightly twisted and shaped into spun sugar decorations for light confectionaries such as iced soufflés, ice-cream and meringue-based puddings. Try coloured spun sugar too.

You will need a sugar boiling thermometer and some liquid glucose, which helps to avoid the graining caused by the scum of impurities that appear on the surface as sugar boils.

You will also need two forks or a balloon whisk with the top, rounded ends of the wire cut off. You should also put several sheets of newspaper on the floor to keep it free of sticky drips.

SPUN SUGAR

Pour 90ml/3½fl oz of water into a pan, then add 250g/9oz of sugar. Stir over a moderate heat until the sugar dissolves and begins to boil. Once it starts to bubble, carefully skim the surface several times and use a wet pastry brush to remove any crystals from the side of the

pan. Add 2½ tbsp glucose, then continue to cook over a high heat. Place the sugar thermometer into the boiling syrup. When it reaches 150°C/305°F, hard crack stage, which means that the syrup becomes brittle and not at all sticky when it is cold. Remove the pan from the heat and rest it on a wooden board for about 1 minute.

To prepare for spinning or throwing the sugar, oil a clean broom handle and anchor one end of it to the work surface, under something like a heavy cast iron casserole, so that it projects over the floor (this is when you need the newspaper on the floor).

Dip the ends of the forks or the cut-down balloon whisk lightly into the syrup. You need only a small amount. With a loose wrist movement, throw it to and fro over the handle. As the syrup is whipped through the air and falls, it is pulled into gossamer-fine threads – the 'spun sugar'. Avoid taking too much syrup at a time because it will cause drips in the threads. When all the syrup is used up, carefully remove the threads from the handle and then gently shape the fine threads in a lightly oiled ring mould. Set this on top of a round iced soufflé or similar dessert, or lightly twisted into smaller shapes for individual sweet dishes.

If it is left at room temperature, spun sugar will start to collapse and disintegrate after about an hour, so it needs to be prepared fairly close to serving. If this seems like a sticky

nightmare, remember it can be prepared at leisure in advance and frozen in a lightly oiled, rigid plastic container until it is needed (see below).

For coloured spun sugar add a few drops of edible food colouring to the pale golden syrup before it reaches the hard crack stage. After the coloured sugar is thrown, the whole can be pulled into small pieces and rolled lightly into balls. The shapes can be stored in a rigid container in the freezer until they are needed. There is no need to defrost them before using them as instant decorations for light desserts.

CARAMEL CAGES

You will need a large chef's ladle, 10cm/4in across, and a little oil.

Rub a thin layer of oil over the back of the ladle, then use a teaspoon to take a little of the hot caramel made as above and let it drop in a thin stream onto the back of the ladle. Just as it drops onto the ladle, start to run the thread backwards and forwards evenly over the ladle. Then take a little more of the caramel and run the threads in a different direction over the mould to form a criss-cross pattern. Leave briefly to get brittle then carefully remove the cage from the ladle by twisting the cage free. Make three more cages in the same way. The caramel in the saucepan will harden before you finish making the other three cages. Return it briefly to the heat until the syrup is the same consistency as before.

QUINCE AND APPLE ROSE TARTLETS IN CARAMEL CAGES

INGREDIENTS
6 sheets of frozen filo pastry, 23 x 25cm/
9 x 10in, defrosted and stacked in 2 piles
of 3 sheets each
25g/1oz melted butter

FILLING
1 tbsp quince jelly
225g/8oz cream cheese
3 small red or green eating apples
lemon juice to prevent discoloration
4 apple roses, made from the skins of
2 apples
4 caramel cages (optional, see page 82)
2 tbsp icing sugar to caramelize the apples

This recipe looks as good as it tastes. The light, crisp filo cases hold a mouth-watering filling of cream cheese mixed with melted quince jelly. If you feel that the caramel decoration is a slightly formidable undertaking serve the tartlets without it. They will still look eye-catching and make the perfect ending to a perfect meal.

Make the filo cases by using a tea cup saucer, 14.5cm/5¾in across, to cut four circles from the three-layered filo. Paint melted butter over the first circle of filo pastry and lay a second circle over the top. Butter this and lay a third circle over these. Press the layered circle into a tartlet tin. Make the other three tartlet bases. Place them over a hot baking sheet in a preheated oven at 190°C/375°F/gas mark 5 for 7 minutes. Leave to cool, then ease the tartlets from the moulds.

Make the filling by melting the quince jelly and mix it into the cheese. Spread about 55g/2oz into each of the cooled case and leave to one side.

Use a sharp knife cut each apple through the centre of the stalk to make halves, then cut these into quarters. Do not peel the apple but remove the core, and cut off a tiny piece from one end of each segment to make a straight edge. Slice the apples very thinly into half-moon shapes, using a mandolin if you have one to make sure that the slices are even. Paint the slices with a little lemon juice to prevent them from discoloration. Arrange the apple slices neatly in a concentric pattern over the surfaces of the filled tartlets, with the little straight ends of the slices facing towards the centre of the tart, leaving a tiny hole in which to place the decoration later.

Dredge over the surfaces of the tartlets with icing sugar and set them on a rack under the grill for 5–6 minutes. Alternatively, use a caterer's torch to caramelize the apples until they are attractively tinged to a dark golden-brown, which emphasizes the pattern of crescents. Add an apple rose to the centre of each tartlet, and decorate each tartlet with a caramel cage. Serve with an extra dusting of icing sugar.

Make the rose decorations from thin strips of apple peel. Roll the strips tightly and secure them with wooden cocktail sticks. Leave in iced, acidulated water for 1 hour before adding one to each tart.

EGG CUSTARD WITH
BAKED RHUBARB COMPOTE

EQUIPMENT
900g/2lb loaf tin or small, individual tins

INGREDIENTS
5 fresh eggs
2½ tbsp caster sugar
600ml/1pt milk
½–1 tsp vanilla essence
¼ tsp freshly grated nutmeg

Creamy egg custards, made with fresh hen's eggs, make delicious country puddings. Eat them on their own or add the lovely tart–sweet flavour of softly poached rhubarb flavoured with angelica (see page 22).

Beat the eggs and sugar in a bowl. Pour over the milk and vanilla essence and whisk them together. Strain through a fine sieve, add the nutmeg, then pour into a lightly greased (with butter) loaf tin or individual tins. Bake in a preheated oven at 100°C/200°F/gas mark ¼ in a bain-marie (a roasting tin half-filled with hot water) for 1½–2 hours. Remove from the oven and leave in the bain-marie until the water is cold. Serve the custard scooped out from the loaf tin or, if you prefer a more elegant presentation, chill overnight in the fridge then turn out and slice before serving. Serve with lightly sweetened poached fruits or with Baked Rhubarb Compote (see below).

BAKED RHUBARB COMPOTE

Cooking rhubarb in this way keeps the red and pink segments whole but still perfectly tender.

EQUIPMENT
1 ovenproof dish

INGREDIENTS
450g/1lb rhubarb
170g/6oz caster sugar
juice of 1 orange
1 branch of 5–6 small to medium angelica leaves

Prepare the rhubarb by cutting off the leaves and trimming the opposite ends. Cut the stalks into 4cm/1½in pieces and place them in a dish. Add the orange juice, angelica and sugar (or honey if you prefer). Stir to distribute the ingredients evenly in the dish, then cover with a lid or with kitchen foil. Bake in a preheated oven at 170°C/325°F/gas mark 3 for 35 minutes. Remove the lid or foil and pour the contents into a pretty china serving dish.

Serve hot or cold, decorated with small sprigs of young angelica leaves, half-pressed into the reddish-pink juices, and with a side dish of chilled cream or clotted cream as an extra luxury.

GOOSE EGG CRÈME BRÛLÉE

SERVES 6

EQUIPMENT
6 large heart-shaped or round ramekins,
7.5cm/3in across

INGREDIENTS
3 goose egg yolks (or 5 chicken egg yolks)
1–2 tbsp milk
110g/4oz vanilla caster sugar
(see page 80)
600ml/1pt double cream
3 tbsp brandy

TOPPING
caster sugar

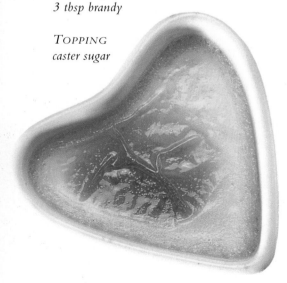

Crème brûlée *is one of everyone's favourite puddings. Few people can resist the thin, brittle caramelized sugar topping set above the rich, velvety goose egg custard (hen's eggs will not produce such a creamy consistency), which should be browned unevenly, so that it ranges from an almost transparent golden to deep brown, rather like the mottled wing of a tortoiseshell butterfly.*

Whisk the eggs well together and strain through a fine sieve into a bowl. Stir in 1–2 tbsp of milk if the yolks are too thick to run through the strainer. Whisk the vanilla sugar into the eggs. Scald the cream and take it off the heat just before it comes to the boil. Pour the cream onto the egg mixture in a thin stream, whisking continually, until they are well combined. Finally, stir in the brandy. Pour the custard into the ramekins and set them carefully in a bain-marie (a roasting tin half-filled with hot water) in a preheated oven at 100°C/200°F/gas mark ¼ for about 1 hour 45 minutes until the custard has set. Leave to cool.

Next make the caramelized topping. Remove the rack from the grill tray and half-fill the tray with a mixture of ice cubes and water. The iced water will help to keep the custard cool and so prevent curdling. Sprinkle 3 level tsp of caster sugar in a thin layer over the surface of each custard and set them in the iced water in the grill tray. Turn the grill full on and grill the custards for 2 minutes or more, depending how far they are from the heat. About 5cm/2in is ideal, and I would suggest between 2 and 2½ minutes under the heat. The surface should look golden to deep brown, and it should be crisp. Alternatively, use a catering torch to caramelize the sugar.

FINISHING OFF

A last-minute dusting of icing sugar produces a simple, dainty finish to a number of sweet dishes, and it can often be more appealing than a more extravagant decoration.

ICING SUGAR

This fine white sugar is widely used in cake-making and confectionary, and it is one of the main ingredients of icing and syrups. Dust if over cakes and pastries to give a professional finish, and it can be used to disguise imperfections such as a cracked top to a sponge cake or a less than perfect pudding.

A simple, soft dusting of the edges of a delicate pudding can emphasize the light texture and subtle flavour of the dish; see Fruits au Gratin with Kummel Custard, page 92, for example. Dusting a tray of feather-light meringues will highlight the contours of the peaks to perfection. Sift icing sugar through a fine mesh sieve over a rich chocolate cake (see Truffes au Chocolat, page 96), or soften the edges of a cut-fruit decoration (see Apple Swan Sorbet, page 76), or use it to pick out the lovely texture and shapes of the almonds and pine nuts scattered over an Italian almond pudding.

A more elaborate decoration can be achieved by placing strips of paper, 1–2cm/½–¾in wide, so that they overlap at regular intervals to make a snowy white criss-cross decoration like lattice-work across the top of a cake or pie. A stencil placed on the surface of a cake can be used to produce a pattern of roses, ivy leaves or perhaps angles and holly leaves for Christmas. One famous chef stencils his favourite patisseries with his initial, and you may want to adapt this idea for your own use.

You can buy ready-made stencils, but with very little trouble and at little expense, you can make your own. Use heavy-weight tracing paper (about 120gsm) to copy a pattern from a book or magazine (children's drawing books are often a good source because they generally have simplified, graphic outlines). Cut out the outline with a craft knife or scalpel, remembering that the bits you cut out will be the areas that will have a snowy pattern when they are dredged with icing sugar.

A square sponge cake is dusted with sifted icing sugar. Use a stencil to make this pretty bow motif.

FRUITS AU GRATIN MADE WITH KUMMEL CUSTARD

SERVES 4

EQUIPMENT
4 round gratin dishes or shallow
soup plates

INGREDIENTS
CUSTARD SAUCE
4 egg yolks
110g/4oz sugar
50ml/2fl oz water
75ml/3fl oz double cream
1½ tbsp kummel

FRUIT
a selection of fresh fruits to include some of
the following: peeled and fanned mango,
pitted cherries, sliced peaches, orange
segments, kiwi fruit (Chinese gooseberries),
seedless grapes, blackberries, sliced banana

This rather spectacular version of fruit and
custard is a very pretty summer dish.
Choose firm, ripe fruit and stud them into
this rich, cream-based custard flavoured with
the heavenly taste of kummel. Do try to use
kummel, which is distilled from caraway
seeds, because it really does taste delicious in
this dish. If you cannot find kummel, use
another fruit-based liqueur instead.

Place the egg yolks, sugar and water in
a bowl set over a pan of gently
simmering water. Whisk for 15–20
minutes or until thick and creamy.
Remove from the heat and continue to
whisk until cold. Fold in the cream
and liqueur.

Peel, stone and slice or fan the fruits,
and set them to one side. Add a pool of
custard to each dish or plate and carefully arrange the fruit in small piles over
the custard. Some but not all of the
fruit will slip into the custard.

Use a catering torch or set the
custard under a hot grill for about 1
minute until the surface looks
appetizingly golden.

Finish off with a chocolate
decoration or a simple sprig of fresh
mint leaves. Serve at once with a fine
dusting of icing sugar, sifted over one
side of the plate to emphasize the
delicacy of this fine dessert.

CHOCOLATE

Chocolate is fun to work with, and if you observe a few simple rules, you can make some truly memorable decorations.

Always use the best quality chocolate. Work in a cool room on a smooth, clean working surface – marble or a large sheet of stainless steel are ideal. Make sure that you have the right equipment: several soft brushes in different sizes; palette knives; strong, straight scrapers (for caraque); and a variety of small moulds, boxes and silicone paper for storage. Above all, make sure you have the time to be creative.

CHOCOLATE DECORATIONS
All the decorations can be stored in a refrigerator or freezer. They should be interleaved with greaseproof or silicone paper and kept in boxes. Begin with 225g/8oz of chocolate and melt more as you need it.

CHOCOLATE LEAVES
When this simple form of decoration is well done, it can be an impressive addition to a multitude of cakes, gateaux and cold puddings. I like to team the chocolate leaves with a moulded chocolate rose. Chocolate leaves look spectacular *en masse* when they are used to embellish a cake. They are especially effective if you mould a variety of shapes in different shades of chocolate.

Use strong, shiny leaves whenever possible – ivy, geranium, bay and rose are suitable. Break dark chocolate into pieces and melt it in a bain-marie of hot water, taken from the heat. Place the bowl of chocolate over the top and leave it to melt. Then stir it until it is smooth. Use a fine artist's paintbrush to coat the chocolate over the top of the leaves. Cover the entire leaf but do not let any chocolate dribble over the edges because this makes peeling difficult. Arrange the leaves, chocolate side up, on a small tray covered in non-stick silicone or greaseproof paper and leave them in the fridge until the chocolate is set. If you prefer the leaves to be slightly curved, lay the freshly coated leaves over a rolling pin wrapped in silicone paper. Leave to set, then add another thin coat of chocolate. Keep the chocolate liquid by standing the bowl over a pan of warm water, reheating it as necessary. Never reheat chocolate over boiling water because the chocolate will look dull and chalky when it sets.

When the chocolate leaves have set, peel the leaf from the chocolate by holding the stem in your fingertips. Store them in a cool, dry place.

ROSE
Mould roses or other flower shapes in the small plastic moulds that can be found in most kitchenware shops and cake-making suppliers. Alternatively, model a rose from small pieces of chocolate marzipan. You can combine a single rose with several curled chocolate leaves to add to the corner of a Sachertorte, the best known of all Viennese cakes, or encircle the top edge of a velvety smooth chocolate gateau or rich chocolate pudding with a garland of leaves and flowers.

CARAQUE
Spread the melted chocolate in the thinnest possible layer over a spotlessly clean working surface. Leave the chocolate to cool and wait until it just begins to set. Test by pressing your fingertips into the edge – they should just leave an impression. Holding your knife or scraper at an angle of 30 degrees, push the knife away from you, gradually straightening it until it is at

90 degrees to the slab. The more acute the angle, the smaller the curls. Take care: if the chocolate sets hard, it will crack as you work. The flakes can be remelted or used to sprinkle between the curls decorating a chocolate roulade, a soufflé or a Black Forest cherry gateau.

PIPED DECORATIONS

You can gain ideas for shapes from all kinds of sources, and many of the designs I have used were traced from children's drawing and painting books.

First, draw or trace small patterns onto a sheet of greaseproof paper. Turn over the paper and lay it on your work surface. Make several small cones from greaseproof paper. Half-fill one with melted chocolate, which should be liquid yet still hold its shape. Snip off the end of the cone and slowly pipe the chocolate in a fine stream onto the paper, following the traced outlines. Leave to set before carefully peeling the shapes away from the paper. Use immediately as for caraque or store them between sheets of silicone paper for later use.

TWO-TONE CHOCOLATE DECORATIONS

Follow the drawn outline of a simple daisy or butterfly with a thin stream of dark chocolate and leave to set. Fill in the petals or wings with milk chocolate and add small blobs of white chocolate to the centre of the flower or to the butterfly's wings.

MOULDING CHOCOLATE

Traditional chocolatiers have always regarded copper moulds as the best. Not only does the metal conduct heat and cold quickly, but copper is softer than other metals and if you exert a little pressure the mould can be made to bend slightly to create an air pocket and so make it easier to release the tempered chocolate. They are, however, expensive. Look around good kitchen ware shops and you are sure to find a good selection of reasonably priced small chocolate moulds made in rigid plastic.

CHOCOLATE DUSTED ALMONDS AND COFFEE BEANS

Dip peeled almonds into smooth melted chocolate, then roll them lightly in a small tray of equal quantities of cocoa and chocolate powder. Leave to dry on silicone or greaseproof paper. Scatter coffee beans coated in melted chocolate over small pots of rich chocolate and brandy mousse.

TRUFFES AU CHOCOLAT

EQUIPMENT
1 tin 17 x 12.5cm/7 x 5in, the base
lined with silicone paper

INGREDIENTS
285g/10oz best quality chocolate
225g/8oz butter
1 tbsp water
1 tbsp caster sugar
2 tbsp rum or brandy
1 dssp Drambuie
2 egg yolks
dusting powder (see opposite)

If time is short for making a dessert, these rich, very dense chocolate truffles will go very well with the coffee, and they are truly luxurious, despite the little time they take to make. For a natural, unfussy presentation, serve them cut into little squares and add a touch of chocolate powder to the icing sugar before dusting over. If you prefer a little extra bitterness, add a little cocoa powder to the dusting mixture.

Remember to use the best quality chocolate and butter for both this recipe and the Keep-your-hands-off Biscuits because their success depends on their rich texture and fine taste.

Place the chocolate, butter, water and sugar in a bain-marie set over hot water (taken from heat) and leave the ingredients to soften. Stir until smooth, then remove the bowl from the heat and leave the mixture to cool a little. Lightly whisk in the alcohol followed by the egg yolks. Pour the mixture into the prepared tin and leave to chill in the fridge for at least 5 hours (preferably overnight).

Remove the slab of chocolate truffle from the tin and peel away the silicone paper. Use a very sharp knife to cut the truffles into small squares and liberally dust with icing sugar mixed with cocoa or chocolate powder. Return to the fridge and serve, straight from the fridge, with coffee.

KEEP-YOUR-HANDS-OFF CHOCOLATE BISCUITS

You need not stint your guests with these scrumptiously gooey chocolate finger biscuits. Like the truffles, they are childishly simple to make and take no time at all. Make them for a special treat for afternoon tea or with morning coffee. If any are left, they will freeze well.

Make the chocolate recipe as for the truffles, but mix in about 40g/1½oz finely crushed digestive biscuits. Then add the same amount of roughly chopped digestive biscuits. Chill and prepare in the same sized tin, but this time cut them into fingers, about 1cm/¾in wide, and dust with icing sugar. Like the truffles, keep them in the fridge until you are ready to serve them.

MARZIPAN MAGIC

Marzipan was first made by nuns in France in the Middle Ages, and it was served as a solid cake. It was originally known as St Mark's pain (pain being French for bread), then as march-pane. In the sixteenth and seventeenth centuries marzipan was considered the ideal material for moulding into the exquisite decorative fantasies that the chefs in the households of royal and noble families created to grace the tables of their patrons. Small, colourful fleur-de-lis, roses, gilded fruits and even family crests were made.

We can follow our ancestors' example and use white marzipan, kneaded with a little food colouring, to make small, sweet decorative shapes, to produce a tray of petits fours or to add to the top of a rich fruit cake instead of fondant. Small marzipan shapes can be coated in melted chocolate or a warm, fluid fondant to make delicious sweets.

BASIC MARZIPAN
225g/8oz caster sugar
225g/8oz icing sugar, sifted
350g/12oz ground almonds
1 tbsp rum or brandy
few drops of vanilla essence
2 large eggs

Place the ingredients in a mixing bowl and combine them with the eggs, beating them lightly to make a moist ball of paste, which is ready to use.

Cut off some of the almond paste and wrap the remaining portion in kitchen film. Place the paste on a working surface, lightly sifted with icing sugar, and knead it until it is perfectly smooth and free from cracks. Divide into small portions and press each one into a small decorative mould, pressing down the top to make the smooth and level.

If the moulds are made of flexible rubber, you can de-mould the shapes immediately, but you will get a better impression if you leave them to chill in the fridge for several hours or in your freezer for 20 minutes.

If your moulds are rigid, you may find it easier to freeze the marzipan inside the mould until it is completely hard. Then press the tip of a small knife between the marzipan and the mould to create an air pocket. Carefully prise the shape out onto silicone paper and leave it to defrost at room temperature. Any small marks can be carefully smoothed over when the paste has softened.

LATTICE MARZIPAN AND MINCEMEAT TARTLETS

This is one of my favourite tartlet recipes, and it shows just how irresistibly delicious cooked marzipan can be. They are perfect at Christmas – serve them warm from the oven, glazed with icing sugar and accompanied by chilled pouring cream.

MAKES 9 TARTLETS

EQUIPMENT
lattice roller cutter (available from good cookware shops)
8cm/3½in biscuit cutter

INGREDIENTS
puff pastry made with 225g/8oz flour
1 jar best quality mincemeat, prepared with rum or brandy
egg glaze
sifted icing sugar for glazing

ALMOND PASTE
225g/8oz ground almonds
110g/4oz icing sugar, sifted
110g/4oz caster sugar
a few drops of almond essence (optional)
whites of 2 eggs, whisked until foamy

Prepare the almond paste as for the Basic Marzipan (see page 98) and leave in the fridge to become firm.

Prepare the puff cases by dividing the pastry into two equal pieces. Wrap one piece in kitchen film and place in the fridge. Roll out the other piece into a square that measures 33 x 33cm/ 13 x 13in.

Divide the almond paste into 9 equal pieces, then roll each piece, with a little icing sugar, in the palms of your hands to form a ball. Lightly flatten the balls into circles with diameters of about 7.5cm/3in and place them on the pastry square, spacing them evenly so that there is about 2.5cm/1in between each circle and from the edges of the pastry to each circle. Slightly raise each disc and place under it 1 rounded tsp of mincemeat. Replace the disc. Lightly paint a little egg wash around each disc. Roll out the second piece of pastry to the same dimensions, then use a cutter to make a lattice pattern the length of the pastry and separate the cuts gently with your fingers to open out the pattern. Carefully roll the pastry around a rolling pin and transfer it to the top of the mincemeat and marzipan. Unroll the pastry slowly and carefully, allowing it to drape so that it covers the mounds. Press around them with your fingertips to seal the pastry, then use a plain biscuit cutter to cut out nine individual tartlets, making sure that the marzipan is in the centre of each circle. Lightly coat the surface of each tartlet with egg glaze then place them on a lightly greased baking sheet. Set this tray on a hot baking sheet to make sure that the base of each pastry cooks thoroughly, then bake in a preheated oven at 220°C/425°F/gas mark 7 for 15 minutes.

Set the tartlets on the grill rack and dredge lightly with icing sugar. Set them under a hot grill and watch as the icing sugar melts and caramelizes into a brittle shine. Be careful because this takes only 1–2 minutes.

FROSTED FRUITS AND LEAVES

Add a sweet and fragile decoration to a light pudding or a sponge cake with small fruits and flowers, finely crusted with sugar. Use small, whole rosebuds, rose petals, herb flower and leaves and fruits such as strawberries, seedless grapes, cherries and jewel-red clusters of redcurrants. Carefully rinse the fruit and leaves and pat them dry with kitchen paper. Use a small paintbrush to give each a fine, even coat of lightly beaten egg white, then dredge with caster sugar. Leave to dry set on non-stick silicone paper in a warm place such as an airing-cupboard or on a sunny windowsill.

ALMOND TUILES, CIGARS AND BISCUITS

MAKES 8 FLOWERS BISCUITS,
14–16 TWIGS, 14 CIGARS

EQUIPMENT
1 prepared baking sheet, lightly greased
with butter, floured then tapped to
release excess flour

INGREDIENTS
25g/1oz home-made marzipan
(see page 98)
or good quality bought marzipan
80g/3oz caster sugar
few drops vanilla essence
1 large egg
65g/2¼ oz flour
pinch of salt
1½ tbsp double cream

This almond paste is ideal for making
decorative sweet containers and biscuits,
which can be moulded over a rolling pin
immediately after being baked, while the
biscuit is still warm and pliable, to make
tuiles (that is, curved like Mediterranean
roof tiles) or to make cups in pretty open
'tulip' shapes. Other decorative shapes –
butterflies, leaves and fleur-de-lis – can be
made by spreading the paste through
stencils, baking and leaving them to cool laid
over curved surfaces, so that they form
delicate three-dimensional shapes. You will
need a scalpel, craft knife or very sharp knife
to cut out the stencils and thin, stiff card,
about 3mm/⅛in thick, which you can buy
from good artists' materials suppliers.

Roughly chop the almond paste and
place it in a mixing bowl or the bowl of
an electric mixer with the sugar, vanilla
essence and egg. Cream the ingredients
with a large spoon or with an electric
beater set at low so that the mixture
does not become frothy. Stir in the flour
and salt until the mixture is smooth and
free from lumps. Cover and leave in the
fridge to rest and become firm for 1
hour. Stir in the cream.

Preheat the oven to 180°C/350°F/
gas mark 4.

To make flowers spread about 2 tsp
of paste thinly over a flower stencil
measuring 20cm/8in across. Cook two
biscuits at a time for about 5 minutes
until they are a pleasing golden-brown
around the edges. Use a palette knife to
loosen each biscuit from the tin while
it is still warm and press it into a small
bowl or brioche tin. So that the biscuits
don't cool and crisp too quickly, I like
to work close to the warmth of the
oven. Continue to prepare the
remaining biscuits.

When the tuiles have cooled and
hardened, carefully remove them from
the moulds and store them in an air-
tight tin. They will keep like this for
several days.

TWIGS

To make twigs, spread 1 tsp of almond paste thinly over the leaf template laid on a prepared tin. Carefully remove the template, taking care that you do not disturb the shaped paste. Bake for 4 minutes. Be very careful when you lift up the leaves because they are very delicate. Lay them over a rolling pin to make a pretty curved leaf.

CHOCOLATE CIGARS

First make the chocolate paste by mixing 1 rounded tbsp of basic almond mixture with 1 tsp of cocoa powder to strengthen the colour. Spoon it into a piping bag with a small no.1 plain piping tube and set to one side.

Spread 1 tsp of almond paste thinly into a circle 10cm/4in across on baking parchment, on which you can draw circles to act as a guide. Alternatively, spread the paste through a round stencil onto the prepared tin. Pipe chocolate paste in a thin stream to make a concentric pattern over the circle of paste.

Cook in batches of four for 4 minutes until the edges look golden. While they are still warm, roll the circles carefully into cigars, the chocolate pattern on the outside, around a narrow metal tube (which you can find in good kitchen ware shops) or something similar. For larger cigars, add a little more almond paste to a circle about 15cm/6in across, when you will have enough for 9–10 biscuits.

BUTTERFLIES

Draw the simple outline of a butterfly on a piece of thin card and cut it out. The size will depend on what you are going to serve them with, but to serve with fruits and ices you should make them about 5–6cm/2–2½in long. Lay the stencil on a ready-prepared baking sheet and spread the mixture thinly and smoothly over it with a small palette knife. A decorator's paint stripping knife is ideal for larger designs. Bake for 3–4 minutes and leave to mould over a curved surface. Pipe a thin line of dark chocolate down the centre of the curve, ending with a bobble for the head and add two thin strips, each ending with a tiny bobble and protruding from the head to simulate the antennae. Alternatively, decorate the butterfly with chocolate almond paste, made as for the cigars (see above), before the biscuits are cooked.

Spiced Wine Cake Decorated with Marzipan

The recipe for this rich fruit cake has been in my family for several generations. Properly made and stored, it is wonderfully delicious and moist.

EQUIPMENT
1 tall 20cm/8in, round cake tin, greased and lined with silicone or greaseproof paper

INGREDIENTS
175g/6oz sultanas
175g/6oz raisins
100g/4oz currants
75g/3oz glacé cherries
75g/3oz mixed peel
150ml/5fl oz sherry
175g/6oz butter
175g/6oz light muscavado sugar
4 eggs (size 2)
100g/4oz self-raising flour
100g/4oz plain flour
pinch of salt
1 level tsp mixed spice
75g/3oz ground almonds
apricot jam, sieved and warmed
½ quantity home-made marzipan (see page 98)

Place the dried fruits into a medium sized mixing bowl with the cherries and the peel. Add the sherry and stir until the fruit is well covered. Cover the bowl with kitchen film and leave for 3 days, turning the fruit every 24 hours to distribute the juices evenly.

Beat the butter and sugar until they are light and creamy. Beat in the eggs. Fold in the flour, salt, spice and ground almonds. Drain the fruit (it will have soaked up most of the sherry, but any excess may be regarded as cook's perks), and stir it lightly into the cake mixture until well blended. Spoon into the prepared tin and carefully smooth the top with a knife.

Bake in a preheated oven at 170°C/325°F/gas mark 3 for 1 hour. Reduce the temperature to 150°C/300°F/gas mark 2 for a further 1½ hours, with the cake loosely covered in foil to prevent it from browning too much. Leave the cake in the tin until it is completely cool. Peel away the lining paper.

Use a pastry brush to paint the cake with the apricot jam. Divide the marzipan into two equal pieces and reserve one piece, wrapped in a plastic bag, for the decorations. Measure up one side of the cake, across the top and down the other side, then roll out the marzipan onto a sheet of greaseproof paper until it is a circle with a diameter slightly larger than this measurement. Invert the whole cake into the centre of the circle and press it gently down so that it sticks evenly over the surface. Turn the cake back the right side and peel away the paper from the marzipan. Smooth over the cake with a rolling pin, carefully working the marzipan into shape around the edge and sides with the palms of your hands. Use a sharp knife to cut off the surplus around the bottom. Carefully slide the cake from your working surface onto your hand, then drop it centrally onto a cake board.

Use the reserved piece of marzipan to make small fruits, flowers and other decorations. Stick them to the surface with a little beaten egg white. If you prefer to use coloured marzipan, add a few drop of food colouring to a tiny ball of marzipan, then use your fingers to knead the small ball into a larger piece. Subtle tones of marzipan look much nicer than bright colours. Wrap the finished cake in soft kitchen paper and store it in an air-tight tin.

CHEESE

Everyone has their own favourite cheeses, and the following are suggestions only, not hard and fast rules. Aim to have an imaginative selection of different categories of cheese, which look good together and which also taste excellent.

If the meal has been fairly complicated and perhaps a little heavy, it is a good idea to offer just one cheese. A good brie is an excellent choice, and a good one to look out for is Brie de Meaux, which is made with unpasteurized cow's milk. It has a smooth, runny texture, like thick cream, and a good flavour. A whole one, which will weigh about 1kg/2lb, will look attractive and will be sufficient for 10–12 people.

If you decide to serve more than one, choose from the following so that you achieve a lovely colour contrast as well as a cheeseboard that covers all the categories of cheese. Try a blue cheese, or a coloured cheese with a splash of orange from the washed rind, a green vine-covered cheese, another decorated with a fern and the lovely white of a plain, ivory-coloured one.

Keeping cheese wrapped in wax paper helps keep them moist yet avoid sweating. Store them in a cold cellar or in a cool room. In hot weather the fridge is best. Bring them into the kitchen about 1 hour before serving to allow the cheese to breath and to gain the maximum flavour and aroma. To prevent them drying unnecessarily, unwrap them just before serving.

A cheeseboard including five or six of the cheeses suggested here would be sufficient for between six and eight people. Arrange the cheeses on a plain board of old wood or cool grey slate or marble, and offer plain wheat wafers or water biscuits. For decoration I would choose only dark grapes or leaves, which can be particularly lovely in autumn when they begin to change colour. These beautiful shapes and colours need no additional embellishment. In winter serve a good claret; a nice, light, crisp Sauvignon Blanc is the perfect accompaniment in summer.

BLUE CHEESE
Choose either Stilton or Roquefort for a smooth, rich flavour with a good tang. The writer Daniel Defoe enjoyed Stilton at the Bell Inn on the Great North Road at Stilton, and he commented on the 'town famous for cheese, which is call'd our English Parmesan'. It has a crinkled, biscuit-coloured crust with a creamy-yellow interior and greenish-blue veining throughout. The sharp flavour should not be too overpowering, and the cheese should have a lovely cream-like texture that melts on the palate.

Roquefort is a semi-soft cheese that is made with ewe's milk. It has a crumbly texture and splashes of bluish-grey veining. It has a strongly salty, almost acidic flavour.

WASHED-RIND CHEESE
Try Petit Langres. This is a cow's milk cheese, which is pressed and washed in salt water to give a real pungency. The rind is a distinctive orange, and the cheese itself has a slightly sticky consistency. It tastes strong and salty and has a pronounced odour. It is a good cheese, nevertheless, which looks something like a Yorkshire pudding.

GOAT'S CHEESE
An attractive cheese is Chabis de Perigord, which makes a nice contrast with the other cheeses because it is wrapped in a vine leaf. There are a lot

of goat's cheese to choose from, all from different small creameries, mostly in France or England, but do look out for this one. It has a smooth, goaty flavour with a hint of citrus. You could also try Fresh Clifton, an English goat's cheese, which is fresh and soft in texture and which has a succulent topping of crystallized ginger. This is a fairly new cheese, but the practice of combining cheese with ginger is well established, possible because ginger is such an excellent digestive.

Decorated Cheese

Choose a bloomy cheese. Fougerus, for example, has a pretty fern decoration set into the rind. It is a cousin of brie, but it has an altogether firmer consistency – soft and creamy around the edges and rather firm and mousse-like in the centre. It has a lovely flavour of fresh mushrooms.

Hard Cheeses

The choice is enormous, but I would suggest a Lancashire, which combines simple charm with a beautifully subtle but fresh taste and a moist, crumbly texture. It simply melts in the mouth, and its stark, creamy white is a lovely contrast to the colours of the other cheeses on the board.

Brittany Cheeses

Served hot, these individual moulded cheeses make an impressive ending to a meal, especially for those who prefer a luxurious savoury nibble of cheese instead of a pudding.

Serves 4

Equipment
4 small, round moulds or 4 impressions in a bun tin

Ingredients
110g/4oz mild English cheddar cheese
2 small cartons of boursin garlic cream cheese
4 thin slices of white bread, cut into squares 6.5 x 6.5cm/2½ x 2½in and with the crusts cut off
small amount of mixed salad leaves, including radicchio for garnish
tomato dressing (see page 30)

Cut the cheddar into four slices, 3–5mm/⅛–¼in thick, and set them on a sheet of greaseproof paper laid over a baking sheet. Place the baking sheet in a moderate oven and after 1½–2 minutes, when the cheese looks soft but not melted, take it out and lift the softened cheese with a palette knife, pressing each piece into a mould or an impression in a bun tin. If the cheese tears, patch it while it is still warm, gently pressing the gaps together with your fingers. Leave to chill and harden in the fridge.

Mash the boursin a little with a fork and fill the centre of the cold cheese moulds. Press the boursin down evenly and smooth over the top, trimming away any ragged edges around the top of the moulds with a sharp knife. Place the tray of cheeses in the freezer until they are solid. Turn them out of the moulds by inserting the tip of a point knife between the cheese and the edge of the mould and gently easing them out. Cover the cheeses and return them to the freezer wrapped in a plastic bag or leave them to defrost slowly in the fridge.

Just before serving, toast the square of bread and warm the cheese briefly, setting them on a baking sheet under a moderate grill until the outer coating begins to melt but retains its domed shape. Use a palette knife to set each cheese on a single piece of toast arranged in the centre of an individual serving plate, encircled with a ring of small torn salad leaves, lightly drizzled over with a little tomato dressing. Sprinkle over some snipped chives and serve immediately. The hot, savoury outer coating of cheddar will reveal a delicious core of soft, melted cheese as it is cut open.

ACKNOWLEDGEMENTS AND CREDITS

I would like to express my special thanks to the editorial and design team at Cassell, particularly to my editor, Christopher Fagg, who made this book possible.

I am very grateful to Alan Ford, Head Chef of Hintlesham Hall, George Street, Hintlesham, near Ipswich, Suffolk IP8 3NS, for advising me on some of the latest food presentation ideas.

I should also like to acknowledge the generosity of the following people and companies, whose help with my research and with products was invaluable: Joan Jones, Curator of the Minton Museum, Royal Doulton, London Road, Stoke-on-Trent, Staffordshire ST4 7QD; Jackie Lesellier, Bagatelle Boutique Patisserie, 44 Harrington Road, London SW7 3NB; Rosemary and Brian Clifton Sprigg, Norfolk Herbs, Blackberry Farm, Dillington, near Gressenhall, East Dereham, Norfolk NR19 2QD; Ben Poole, Imperial Teas of Lincoln, Steep Hill, Lincoln LN2 1LU; Martin Wick and Denise Smith, The Fromagerie, Harrods, London SW1 7XL; Andrew Bown, wine expert, for his contribution on the uses of wine and liqueurs in cooking; Julian Tomkins, La Maison des Sorbets, 51–55 St Thomas Street, London SE1 3QX; Brian Nutman, Couverture, Leathams Larder, Bethwin Road, Camberwell, London SE5 0BB; Paul Goodfellow, Continental Chef Supplies for Professional Kitchen Equipment, Unit 11, South Hetton Industrial Estate, South Hetton, Co. Durham DH6 2EU; Sue Moore, Cranes Watering Farm Dairy, Starston, Norfolk.

I should also like to thank the following suppliers for the loan of the following products: Paperchase, 213 Tottenham Court Road, London W1P 9AF (paper); Osborne & Little, 304–308 Kings Road, London SW3 (wallpapers); Pierre Frey, 251–253 Fulham Road, London SW3 6HY (materials); Farrow & Ball, National Trust Paints, 33 Uddens Trading Estate, Uddens Cross, Wimborne, Dorset BH21 7NL (paints); David Mellor, 4 Sloane Street, London SW1V 8EE (kitchen equipment): Small Holding Supplies, Pike Farmhouse, East Pennard, Shepton Mallet, Somerset BA4 6RR (dairy appliances); Russells of Dereham, 19 Market Place, East Dereham, Norfolk NR19 2AX (cake making equipment); Isis Ceramics, The Old Toffee Factory, Oxford OX1 4LS (blue scalloped china dish used in the jacket shot).

I should like to express my grateful thanks for the beautiful antique china and furniture that was so generously loaned for photography by the following shops: Beverley, Art Nouveau, Art Deco, 30 Church Street, Marylebone, London NW8 8BP; Richard Scott of Richard Scott Antiques, 30 High Street, Holt, Norfolk NR25 6BH; Kim Sisson and Jane Cudlip, Friend or Faux, 28 Earsham Street, Bungay, Suffolk NR35 1AG.

My thanks, too, to illustrator Josephine Marston, who allowed me to use her lovely home as an instant 'props' house.

Finally, thanks to Richard and Jenita Nemar-Smith at Reflections Professional Colour Laboratory, 4 Beckham Place, Edward Street, Norwich NR3 3DZ, for processing the films so efficiently and for their help throughout.

INDEX